Anti-Pluralism

Anti-Pluralism

The Populist Threat to
Liberal Democracy

William A. Galston

Foreword by James Davison Hunter and John M. Owen IV

Yale UNIVERSITY PRESS

New Haven & London

Published with the assistance of the
Institute for Advanced Studies in Culture, University of Virginia, and with
assistance from the Louis Stern Memorial Fund.

Portions of chapter 1 originally appeared in William A. Galston,
"The 2016 U.S. Election: The Populist Moment," *Journal of Democracy*
(April 2017): 21–33.

Yale University Press books may be purchased in quantity for educational,
business, or promotional use. For information, please e-mail
sales.press@yale.edu (U.S. office) or sales@yaleup.co.uk (U.K. office).

Set in Janson Roman type by Integrated Publishing Solutions,
Grand Rapids, Michigan.
Printed in the United States of America.

Library of Congress Control Number: 2017952044
ISBN 978-0-300-22892-2 (hardcover : alk. paper)

A catalogue record for this book is available from the British Library.

This paper meets the requirements of ANSI/NISO Z39.48-1992
(Permanence of Paper).

10 9 8 7 6 5 4 3 2 1

To Václav Havel and Liu Xiaobo, who never lost hope

Contents

Contents

Foreword

The Yale University Press series Politics and Culture begins with the premise that self-government, the hallmark and glory of the United States, the West, and an expanding number of countries around the world, is ailing. Those who sense the ailment cannot agree on what it is, much less on how it is to be treated; and that disagreement, only deepening as time passes, is in fact part of the ailment. In the young twenty-first century, liberal democracy, that system that marries majority rule with individual rights, has entered a crisis of legitimacy. As practiced in recent decades, and as an international ordering principle, it has failed to deliver on its promises to growing, and increasingly diverse, numbers of mobilized and vocal people. The fate of liberal democracy would seem to be in the balance.

In the United States and across Europe, the discontented have multiplied, sorting themselves into political factions that are new, yet familiar too. Populisms of right and left, fed and channeled by new media, threaten to upend liberalism's grand ambition to pull down all barriers to individual autonomy or emancipation. In recent decades, for example, liberalism has become allied with the forces of globalization and, in the process, has eroded barriers of national sovereignty with the free movement of goods, capital, and even people across national boundaries. This has generated all sorts of dislocations, most obviously in local economies and labor markets. Just as important, though, are cultural dislocations driven by the growing dominance of a secular, progressive cosmopolitanism that has acted like a solvent on local cultures. All of this carries disruptive political consequences on the left and on the right that have no obvious solutions. It is the absence of substantive political solutions that seem fair and just that explains why (among other reasons) such large swathes of the public are so restive.

William Galston is rightly known as one of the most astute political observers writing today. He is both a political theorist and a policy analyst and is equally at home in both worlds. In *Anti-Pluralism* he draws together a synthesis of philosophical insight, historical evidence, and empirical data in a cogent analysis of the complex difficulties facing liberal democracy in the early twenty-first century. Liberal democracy can survive its legitimation crisis, he argues, but its preservation requires its reform, and reformation requires reflection on what is to be preserved and what accretions and by-products of actually existing liberalism need to be shed. Readers of his previous books will recognize the fairness and judgment on display here. Any repair of the liberal project will require the kind of critical response Professor Galston mounts: he consults the sources, observes carefully, and proposes reforms large and small, listening throughout to all citizens, regardless of circumstance or conviction.

James Davison Hunter and
John M. Owen IV, Series Editors

Acknowledgments

My thanks go first to the University of Virginia's Institute for Advanced Studies in Culture and especially to James Davison Hunter and John M. Owen IV, who hosted the paper that launched me on this path and then the lectures at the University of Virginia that moved me down the path toward this book. Their steadfast support over the past four years was indispensable.

Second, I must thank my colleagues at the Brookings Institution —too numerous to list—for their willingness to share with me the fruits of their research. I have learned from Brookings scholars in economics, foreign policy, and metropolitan studies as well as in my home base in governance studies. The mélange of disciplines and methods this book employs reflects their influence and is the better for it. In an era of academic hyperspecialization, Brookings represents a genuine intellectual community.

I must express my gratitude to Clara J. Hendrickson, who began as my research assistant and ended as my collaborator. Her ability to assemble, digest, and summarize large quantities of material was invaluable. Her talents as editor and critic improved every page of this book. And she wrote with a maturity beyond her years, so much so that I entrusted her with the first draft of chapter 4. I am not sure I would have finished this book without her; I know her efforts made it better. Needless to say, I bear ultimate responsibility for all its remaining sins, whether of commission or omission.

I am grateful, finally, to Oxford University Press and Johns Hopkins University Press for permission to make use of previously published materials.

Anti-Pluralism

Challenges to Liberal Democracy

In just twenty-five years, the partisans of liberal democracy have moved from triumphalism to near despair. Neither sentiment is warranted. History is not a linear movement toward a liberal democratic world. Liberal democracy is not the end of history; nothing is. Everything human beings make is subject to erosion and contingency. Liberal democracy is fragile, constantly threatened, always in need of repair.

But liberal democracy is also strong, because, to a greater extent than any other political form, it harbors the power of self-correction. Not only do liberal democratic institutions protect citizens against tyrannical concentrations of power, they also provide mechanisms for transforming the public's grievances and unmet needs into effective reforms. These mechanisms do not run on their own; they need determined leaders with clear ideas. Fortunately, they permit such leaders to gain power: witness the astonishing victory of French president Emmanuel Macron, who upended an ossified system and heads a parliamentary majority party that did not even exist two years ago.

To be sure, the power of self-correction is not always enough to prevent liberal democracies from crumbling. As we learned in the 1920s and 1930s, the combination of public stress and strong undemocratic movements can be irresistible. But the oft-heard analogy between those decades and our current situation obscures more than it reveals. Today's economic ills pale in comparison to the Great Depression of the 1930s, and today's autocratic regimes lack the ideological power that fascism and communism enjoyed at their peak.

The inaptness of this comparison is no cause for complacency. The current ills of liberal democracy are deep and pervasive. Surmounting them will require intellectual clarity and political leaders who are willing to risk their careers to serve the long-term interests of their countries. Human choice, not historical inevitability, will determine liberal democracy's fate. For now, democratic publics only want policy changes that give them hope for a better future. Left unmet, their demands could evolve into pressure for regime change.

When I began writing about the travails of liberal democracy a few years ago, I believed economics represented the heart of the matter. Contemporary liberal democracy, I argued, rested on a tacit compact between peoples on the one hand and their elected representatives and unelected experts on the other. The people would defer to elites as long as elites delivered sustained prosperity and steadily improving living standards. If they stopped managing the economy effectively, all bets were off.

This compact began to weaken with growing competition from developing nations, which put pressure on policies designed to protect citizens against labor market risks. In many Western democracies, the erosion of the manufacturing sector destabilized regions and political arrangements. The urbanization of opportunity—the shift of economic dynamism away from smaller communities and rural areas toward a handful of metropolitan areas—intensified these effects. Inequality rose. A globalized economy, it turned out, served the interests of most people in developing countries and elites in advanced countries—but not the working and middle classes in the developed economies, which had done so well in the three decades after World War II.

Against this backdrop, the Great Recession following December 2007 represented a colossal failure of economic stewardship, and leaders' inability to restore vigorous economic growth compounded the felony. (A McKinsey Global Institute study found that 81 percent of U.S. households, 70 percent of U.K. households, and 97 percent of Italian households had experienced declining incomes since 2005.)[1] As economies struggled and unemployment persisted, the groups and regions that failed to rebound lost confidence in mainstream parties and established institutions, fueling the populist upsurge that upended American politics, threatened the European Union, and challenged liberal governance itself in several of the newer democracies.

While this account is not wrong, I now believe it represents only a portion of the truth. An explanation that places economics at the base and treats other issues as derivative distorts a more complex reality. Alongside economic difficulties, other problems weakened the foundation of popular support for established institutions.

For example, the United States, the United Kingdom, and the European Union all failed to deal with waves of immigration in ways that commanded public support. Not only did immigrants compete with longtime inhabitants for jobs and social services, they were also seen as threatening long-established cultural norms and even public safety. The spread of higher education created new cultural divisions: a college degree not only expands economic opportunities but also reshapes individuals' entire outlook. College graduates tend to be less wedded to traditional norms, more comfortable with rapid change, and more accepting of diversity. Many less educated citizens came to feel that their lives were outside their control, not only individually but also collectively. The national and international governing institutions they thought would step in when individual agency proved insufficient seemed frozen as leaders stalled and bickered. Many citizens lost confidence in the future and longed instead for an imagined past that insurgent politicians promised to restore. In the United States, partisan polarization gridlocked the system, preventing progress on problems that demanded concerted action. In Europe, the opposite phenomenon—a center-left/center-right duopoly that kept important issues off the public agenda—had much the same effect.

Liberal democracy has two characteristic deformations. Elitists claim that they best understand the means to the public's ends and should be freed from the inconvenient necessity of popular consent. They regard themselves as the defenders of liberal values, but they have doubts about democracy. They are sure that they are promoting the public interest, but they understand it through the prism of their own class interests and biases. Their efforts to insulate themselves from the people—in the quasi-invisible civil service, in remote bureaucracies, in courts and international institutions—inevitably breed resentment.

The result has been liberal democracy's other deformation: the rise of populist movements—and in several cases governments—across the West. Some observers argue that populism is a vacuous category, the omnibus label for everything educated elites despise. I disagree: populism is a form of politics that reflects distinctive theoretical commitments and generates its own political practice. Populists view themselves as arch-democrats who oppose what they regard as liberalism's class biases. Their majoritarianism puts pressure on the individual rights and the limits on public power at the heart of liberal democracy. More dangerous still is the populists' understanding of the "people" as homogeneous and unitary, which leans against the pluralism that characterizes all free societies in modernity. Because the assumption of homogeneity is always false, it leads first to denial and then to suppression. Faced with disagreement, populism responds with anathemas: the dissenters are self-interested, power-hungry elites who aren't part of the virtuous and united people. They are rather the enemies of the people and deserve to be treated as such.

Even this more complex account still does not suffice to explain the worrying retreat of liberal democracy. A quarter century ago, it was possible to believe that all serious alternatives had faded and that liberal democracy would continue its inexorable global advance. Ensuing developments have dispelled this dangerous complacency. Autocracy, ethnonationalism, messianic religion, and China's brand of market-Leninism are all advancing while claiming superiority to self-government by popularly elected representatives. Liberal democracy addresses many human desires, but not all of them.

Nonetheless, there is much that liberal democratic governments can do to mitigate their insufficiencies. Public policy can mitigate the heedlessness of markets and slow unwanted change. Nothing requires democratic leaders to give the same weight to outsiders' claims as to those of their own citizens. They are not obligated to support policies that weaken their working and middle classes, even if these policies improve the lot of citizens in developing countries. They are certainly not obligated to open their doors to all newcomers, whatever the consequences for their citizenry. Moderate self-preference is the moral core of a defensible nationalism. Unmodulated internationalism will breed—is breeding—its antithesis, an increasingly unbridled nationalism.

While today's problems are distinctive, they are hardly unique. Nor are they temporary. The basic structure of liberal democracy creates tensions that can never be expunged. At best they can be managed in response to ever-changing circumstances.

Liberal democracy rests on a foundation of a broadly accepted tolerance that asks a good deal of citizens but undermines itself when pushed too far. It stands in a distinctive relation to truth, freely sought and freely discussed, as the requisite for social freedom and sound policy. But unscrupulous forces can abuse this freedom for their own advantage. Demagogy is democracy's shadow.

Liberal democracy needs leaders who eschew the extremes of populism and elitism. They should not pander, but neither should they substitute their own ends for those that the people espouse. Their task is to find effective means for achieving public goals while helping the people better understand their long-term interests.

Although liberal democracy is the most capacious form of political organization, it is not equally hospitable to all ways of life. Its individualism cannot meet the craving for intense and persisting communal solidarity. For some, its antiheroic culture lacks nobility, and its egalitarianism devalues excellence. Its politics, which tends toward incremental compromise and the conciliation of diverse interests, leaves the desire to revolutionize an imperfect world unsatisfied. It represses some permanent features of human psychology—the tendencies toward cruelty and aggression and what Augustine termed the *libido dominandi*. Individuals who crave social stability must look elsewhere, as must those who experience individual freedom and responsibility as burdens rather than blessings.

Civilization, Freud reminded us, always has its discontents, and liberal democracy is no exception. But every other form of political organization is worse, and the friends of liberal democracy should not be shy about saying so.

ONE

Democratic Erosion and Political Convergence

"American exceptionalism" is a sturdy if contested trope. But large changes in American politics since the end of World War II have been anything but exceptional. Rather, the United States has moved in tandem with other Western democracies.

In the three decades following the war, democracies on both sides of the Atlantic built systems of social provision and protection, which Europeans call social democracy and Americans the welfare state. A broad consensus across party lines supported this policy. In the United States, Republican President Dwight Eisenhower ended his party's effort to roll back the New Deal, and Republican President Richard Nixon expanded the federal government's activities in virtually every domain of social policy. As inflation surged, Nixon outraged devotees of the free market by imposing wage and price controls.

Starting in the mid-1970s, the expansion of the welfare state slowed amid rising concerns about its impact on public finances and private-sector growth. "The Crisis of Democracy," a much-discussed

Trilateral Commission report published in 1975, went on at length about democratic "overload"—public demands exceeding the government's capacity to finance and administer them.[1]

The intellectual and political forces opposed to the welfare state helped bring about the second political convergence of the postwar era—conservative retrenchment—led by Ronald Reagan and Margaret Thatcher. Retrenchment was not reversal. Reagan did not seriously challenge core social insurance programs such as Social Security and Medicare, and Thatcher left the United Kingdom's iconic National Health Service largely intact. But they did raise doubts about government's competence, and they reinvigorated market mechanisms as models for the public as well as the private sector. The reoriented Republican Party in the United States and the Conservative Party in the United Kingdom each won three consecutive national elections.

Across the Channel, Christian Democrat Helmut Kohl became the chancellor of West Germany in 1982, after thirteen years of Social Democratic dominance, and proceeded to cut public expenditures, reduce regulations, and privatize public holdings. Even France's François Mitterrand, who came to power in 1981 on a bold program of expanding socialism, was forced to execute a U-turn toward austerity after less than two years in office. During his presidency, moreover, he twice had to cohabit with conservative prime ministers whose parties prevailed in parliamentary elections.

Confronted with resurgent conservatism, reform-minded leaders worked to renovate left-leaning parties. This brought the next convergence of Western politics, the Third Way. Bill Clinton led the charge, becoming president in 1993 as leader of the New Democrat movement within the Democratic Party. Inspired by Clinton's example, a New Labour team clustered around Tony Blair and Gordon Brown revived the British Labour Party, replacing its hard-edged socialism and pacifism with an internationalist and market-friendly agenda. The remodeled Labour Party swept the Conservatives from power in 1997 and went on to win national elections in 2001 and again in 2005. In 1998, Gerhard Schröder, the leader of the Social Democratic Party, became Germany's chancellor and worked successfully to modernize social welfare policies, reduce taxes, and reform his country's labor market, helping to lay the foundation for a German economic revival after years of slow growth.

For some years, international Third Way forces had the wind in their sails. The fall of the Berlin Wall and the implosion of the Soviet Union signaled not only the end of the twentieth century's last remaining ideological challenge to liberal democracy but also the more rapid integration of the global economy. At first, Western countries were well positioned to take advantage of this emerging reality, and the "Washington consensus"—which included fiscal discipline, pro-growth public investment, liberalization of trade and investment, and deregulation—became canonical for developed as well as developing countries.

The Great Recession ended this era. Across the West, governments struggled to stave off financial collapse, halt the downward slide of output and employment, and restart economic growth. Advocates of austerity battled with supporters of stimulus. Even when growth resumed—earlier in the United States than elsewhere, earlier in northern than southern Europe—it was too slow and uneven to meet public expectations.

This brings us to the present, to the fourth—and most troubling —convergence of postwar democratic politics. From Mitteleuropa to England's Midlands to the American Midwest, a revolt has developed against the arrangements that have shaped the democratic West since the fall of the Berlin Wall and the collapse of the Soviet Union. A populist surge threatens the assumptions and achievements of mainstream politicians and policymakers from the center-left to the center-right. Economic policies based on free trade and flexible labor markets came under attack. Cultural norms celebrating diversity and promoting immigration lost traction. International agreements and institutions yielded ground to nationalist forces.

Although the Great Recession helped set the stage, these discontents were exacerbated by surges of migration across Europe in response to civil war in Syria and drought in Africa. The failure of past reforms to stem the tide of illegal immigration had similar consequences in the United States.

But larger forces are at work. Technological change has triggered new modes of production and a shift toward more knowledge-intensive economies, weakening mass manufacturing throughout the West. These forces have also catalyzed the rise of an education-based meritocracy that dominates government, the bureaucracy, the media, and major metropolitan areas. The emergence of this new elite has left less educated citizens in outlying towns and rural areas feeling denigrated and devalued, sowing populist resentment. As David Goodhart vividly puts it, these economic and social developments have divided democratic citizenries into "Anywheres"—individuals whose identities are professional and who can use their skills in many places, at home and abroad—and "Somewheres"—individuals whose identities are tightly bound to particular places where their forebears have lived for generations.[2]

These trends are deepening social divisions: between more and less educated citizens; between those who benefit from technological change and those who are threatened by it; between the cities and the countryside; between long-established groups and newer entrants into the civic community; between those who celebrate dynamism and diversity and those who prize stability and homogeneity. Elites' preference for open societies is running up against public demands for economic, cultural, and political closure.

But the challenge goes even deeper. Some parties on the left and the right are calling into question the norms and institutions of liberal democracy itself, especially freedom of the press, the rule of law, and the rights of minorities. Throughout the West there is rising impatience with governments that seem incapable of acting forcefully to deal with mounting problems. Rising insecurity has triggered a demand for strong leaders, risking a return to forms of authoritarianism that many thought had been left behind for good.

To be sure, there are signs that liberal democracy's capacity for self-correction is beginning to stir. In France, Marine Le Pen lost the presidential contest by a margin of two to one to a dynamic young centrist politician whose new En Marche! party then won an absolute parliamentary majority. In the United Kingdom, Theresa May's snap election blew up in her face, forcing her to soften her stance on Brexit and compromise with the 48 percent of British voters who wanted to remain within the European Union. In the United States, the system of separated powers has curbed the newly elected populist president's most serious challenges to the constitutional order. A heightened sense of the need for change has spread throughout the West's established democracies.

None of this means that liberal democracy is out of the woods. Its defenders have been given a reprieve, not a pardon. It remains to be seen whether they will prove equal to the occasion. And the clock is ticking. Marine Le Pen's father, the first National Front candidate to reach the final round of a French presidential election, received only 17 percent of the vote. In 2017, Mme. Le Pen doubled his share. If Emmanuel Macron fails to revitalize France's economy and narrow the breach between its thriving metropolitan areas and declining manufacturing regions, the National Front could be France's future. In several of Europe's postcommunist countries, elected governments are weakening liberal institutions. And there is no way to know how U.S. voters will react if Donald

Trump cannot honor his campaign promises to reopen coal mines and steel mills, revitalize the manufacturing sector, and reverse the declining fortunes of the Rust Belt and small-town America.

Empirical evidence reveals clear signs of democratic erosion during the past decade. Between 1974 and 2006, electoral democracies rose from 29 percent to 61 percent of governments around the world, and liberal democracies from 21 percent to 41 percent. Then the democratic surge ended, and the tide has ebbed ever since. The year 2016 was the eleventh straight year in which countries suffering net declines in political and civil liberties outnumbered the gainers. In nearly all these years, the losses substantially exceeded the gains.[3]

More broadly, this period has seen a decline in the quality of democracy, as measured by political rights, civil liberties, transparency, and the rule of law. Between 1986 and 2006, the share of countries with political and civil freedoms rose from 34 percent to 47 percent, and the share without them fell from 32 percent to 23 percent. Between 2006 and 2016, the share of free countries fell from 47 percent to 45 percent, while the share without freedoms rose from 23 percent to 25 percent. And there has been an alarming shift in the locus of decline. As the annual report "Freedom in the World 2017" puts it, "While in past years the declines in freedom were generally concentrated among autocracies and dictators that simply went from bad to worse, in 2016 it was established democracies . . . that dominated the list of countries suffering setbacks."[4] There were signs of decline in Hungary, Poland, and even France. Many observers have begun to worry about the strength of democratic institutions even in the United States. There is broad agreement that the energy, efficacy, and self-confidence of the world's democracies and the forces supporting democratic expansion have waned.

Democracy faces a renewed external challenge—the authoritarian surge. This phenomenon may have begun as a defensive response to the wave of "color revolutions" that began in Georgia in 2003 and spread to Ukraine, Belarus, and elsewhere before reaching Iran in the Green Revolution of 2009. But it was not long before Russia, China, and Iran went on the offensive, bringing new states into their spheres of influence. Cooperation among these and other authoritarian governments has increased. Countries with deep pockets, especially China and the Gulf States, used their financial reserves to diminish pro-democratic threats and strengthen friendly nondemocratic regimes. Many autocrats have attacked civil society institutions, especially those with substantial funding from abroad. Russia has aggressively used cyberattacks and disinformation campaigns to weaken established democracies and even influence their elections.

Although the authoritarian surge has put pressure on democratic countries and movements, internal challenges are likely to prove more consequential. These challenges begin as opposition to decades-old policies of liberal democracies such as free trade, international institutions, and relative openness to immigrants and refugees. In countries where traditional values remain strong, segments of the population oppose liberal social policies (especially concerning gender relations and same-sex marriage) and movement toward what they regard as secularism. Often this opposition takes the form of antipathy to political, economic, and cultural elites.

Patrick Chamorel's study of Marine Le Pen's National Front (FN) vividly portrays this ensemble of developments: "A majority of FN supporters reject the right/left dichotomy and what they see as an altogether corrupt political class that goes with it. They believe that France is in deep decline, has too many immigrants, and needs a strong leader to restore order. For many of them, the world is changing too fast and in the wrong direction, and they perceive a need for the state to protect them. The party's inclination is to bring back an idealized past more than to invent a radically new social order. It nurtures a traditionalist and Catholic proclivity and yet is split on gay marriage. . . . In foreign policy, it is not unlike the former 'paleo-conservatives' of Pat Buchanan in the United States, with an isolationist, protectionist, anti-immigration, and traditionalist message."[5]

None of this necessarily threatens liberal democracy. "Strong" leaders—Winston Churchill, Franklin Roosevelt, Charles de Gaulle —have often been fully compatible with representative institutions and respect for individual rights. In dark times, they can be essential for the preservation of liberal democracy. But sometimes the yearning for strong leadership gives rise to antidemocratic sentiments. "Like so many European extremist parties," Chamorel observes, "the Front National has expressed its admiration for Vladimir Putin's nationalist and traditionalist values, his cult of order and authoritarian leadership."[6]

These developments are taking place against a backdrop of mounting threats to the postwar liberal democratic order. Since the end of World War II, a bargain between political leaders and citizens has defined this order's perimeter. Working through bureaucracies, popularly elected governments would deliver economic growth and rising living standards; social protections for health, employment, and retirement; domestic tranquillity; and the abatement of international threats. In return, the people would defer to political elites.

For half a century after the war, the bargain held, and public support for both liberal democracy and its leaders remained high. But as governments have failed to deliver their end of the bargain, public confidence has waned. While for some people liberal democracy may be an intrinsic good, an end in itself, for most it is a means to prosperous, peaceful, and secure lives. It is a tree known by its fruit. If it ceases to produce the expected crop, it can be cut down.

The decades of sustained and inclusive economic growth after World War II have given way to slower growth, much higher unemployment, and stagnant wages. Throughout the West, democratic governments failed to address the fallout from the Great Recession, and public discontent swelled accordingly. The United States, where the recession began at the end of 2007, did better than most. Nevertheless, its economic recovery was the weakest in decades, averaging just 2 percent GDP growth per year, and household incomes are no higher than they were at the end of the 1990s. Although growth has finally resumed in the European Union, its pace is muted, and unemployment, though declining, remains elevated by historical standards.

Growth, such as it is, has been unbalanced. Some sectors have boomed while others have languished. Global competition has hit mining and manufacturing especially hard, with predictable effects on the regions heavily dependent on these industries. Throughout the West, working-class citizens are in full revolt against these developments. Few governments have found effective remedies for the downsides of globalization and technological change, and political leaders' reluctance even to acknowledge them has added insult to injury.

Equally pervasive is the growing gap between metropolitan areas on the one hand and smaller communities and rural areas on the other. Most cities are thriving; most smaller towns are not. At one time, the fortunes of large cities and their hinterlands were linked; now cities are like black holes, absorbing skilled labor and resources while emitting neither wealth nor opportunity to surrounding areas.

The challenges to liberal democracy go well beyond economics. Waves of immigration have aroused fears that national identities will be irreversibly altered. As demography shifts, "old stock" citizens fear a loss of status and cultural centrality. The perception that immigrants are winning the battle for scarce social resources has made matters worse. Antipathy to minorities, domestic and foreign-born, has intensified.

There are fears, moreover, of attacks by immigrants and refugees harboring terrorist sentiments. The consequence is a demand for unattainable levels of security. Governments face the delicate task of protecting their citizens without abandoning liberal commitments to the rule of law. Balancing the interests of citizens against the claims of migrants facing economic hardship and political persecution is equally challenging, and many governments have failed this test.

The cultural cleavage between cities and the countryside is as old as human history, but recent events have exacerbated it. Urban dwellers tend to prize heterogeneity and dynamism, while people in small towns and rural areas prefer homogeneity and stability. Cities lean toward social liberalism, nonurban areas toward tradition. Religion, especially conservative religion, tends to be stronger in the countryside. City folk often regard the residents of rural communities and small towns as country bumpkins, uneducated and unsophisticated, generating a backlash against elites who are seen as lacking respect for their fellow citizens.

Broader political trends have contributed to democratic erosion. After the fall of the Berlin Wall and the collapse of the Soviet Union, the range of political debate in the West narrowed. As economic globalization and international institutions became the lingua franca of political discourse, center-left and center-right parties converged. In several countries they came together in "grand coalitions."

This consensus politics proved workable as long as favorable economic and security conditions prevailed. But when the tide started turning in 2008, established parties and institutions found it difficult to respond to rising public discontent. Gridlock preserved a status quo that more and more citizens found unacceptable. They grew impatient with political arrangements that seemed incapable of responding boldly, and their frustration found outlets in new, often marginal political parties whose leaders promised more effective institutional arrangements, even at some cost to democracy.

The unpopular, ineffective response of international institutions to economic and refugee crises contributed to a resurgence of nationalism in many parts of the West. The United Kingdom's stunning decision to leave the European Union was a sign of this, as was Donald Trump's "America First" foreign policy. In Central and Eastern Europe, long-muted nationalist sentiments resurfaced.

Although nationalism has often led to antidemocratic changes, these developments do not necessarily represent an erosion of democracy. The vote for Brexit, for example, was a peaceful exercise of democratic decision-making. Many British citizens said they voted to leave the European Union in order to regain democratic self-government, which they thought had been surrendered to unelected bureaucrats in Brussels. The rising nationalist tide in Poland and Hungary, on the other hand, does pose a threat to liberal democracy. The American presidential election is hard to assess, and its effects on American institutions are harder to predict.

Looking back, it is difficult to avoid concluding that democratic elites were complacent. Scholars thought that once countries had reached a certain level of economic development and had made the transition to democracy, they would never turn back. After the epochal events of the late 1980s and early 1990s, Francis Fukuyama discerned the "end of history"—the disappearance of serious alternatives to liberal democracy. Systems that combined representative institutions with protections for individual and minority rights were the only game in town, or so it seemed.

The economic and governance failures of Russia's new democracy represented the first blow to this optimistic narrative. China's remarkable economic surge showed that market mechanisms were not necessarily incompatible with authoritarian politics. The erosion of the manufacturing sector throughout much of the West accelerated working-class disaffection, and the painfully slow recovery from the financial crisis and ensuing Great Recession created an opening for new political voices, many of which evinced little sympathy for liberal democracy.

When democratization was on the march, the liberal world order was strong and self-confident. The message to countries emerging from economic stagnation and political repression was clear: join the winners, because we can give you moral and material support during your difficult transition to open economies and democratic self-government. As authoritarian governments went on the offensive and democratic self-confidence waned, this message lost some credibility. If the world's most powerful democracy continues to challenge such institutions as NATO, the European Union, and the World Trade Organization, this trend may well intensify.

The spread of democracy in successive waves after the end of World War II took place under an international canopy of incentives and protections. If liberal democracies are to regain their élan, democratic leaders must find ways to re-create the international environment that allowed self-government to flourish.

TWO

Liberal Democracy in Theory

When we worry about "liberal democracy," it helps to know what we are talking about. In this chapter I distinguish, and then connect, four concepts—the republican principle, democracy, constitutionalism, and liberalism.

The Republican Principle

By the republican principle I mean popular sovereignty or, more formally, the people as the sole source of legitimacy. Otherwise put, only the people can rightly authorize forms of government. This idea is at the heart of the most American of all documents, the Declaration of Independence, which famously asserts, "Governments are instituted among men, deriving their just powers from the consent of the governed." When a specific form of government no longer promotes the ends for which it was established, the people may withdraw their consent and establish a new type of government that they consider more likely to attain these ends.

There is no direct link between popular sovereignty and any

particular form of government, including democracy; the people may authorize a range of regimes. In his inauguration speech in 1933, Franklin Roosevelt said that if existing institutional forms did not suffice to surmount the economic crisis, he would ask Congress and the American people for emergency powers. Consistent with the Declaration, James Madison says: "We may define a republic to be . . . a government that derives all its powers directly or indirectly from the people." In a republic, he continues, "It is *essential* to such a government that it be derived from the great body of society, not from an inconsiderable proportion or a favored class of it."[1]

Though popular sovereignty guides republican thought, the people do not always run the institutions they create. Nor are they always the fount of wisdom. "The people commonly *intend* the public good," Alexander Hamilton asserts, but they do not always "*reason right*" about the *means* of promoting it."[2] Closing the gap between intent and wisdom is a central challenge to republican institution-making. We are no longer as sure as Madison was that stable self-government requires the "*total exclusion of the people in their collective capacity*" from actual governance.[3]

The Declaration's opening sentence assumes the existence of a distinct "people" with the right to dissolve its connection with another people. But who or what is "the people"? This may sound like an abstract, theoretical question. It is anything but.

We now understand "We the people" as all of us—all citizens, regardless of religion, manners and customs, and length of citizenship. The people is an ensemble of individuals who enjoy a common civic status. Publius, however, articulates a thicker understanding. John Jay writes in *Federalist* No. 2 that "Providence has been pleased to give this one connected country to one united people—a people descended from the same ancestors, speaking the same language, professing the same religion, attached to the same principles of government, very similar in their manners and customs."[4] There is reason to doubt whether Jay's description of the American people was ever true. (It certainly isn't now.) The question is why he felt impelled to push the argument in this direction. The answer, I suggest, is that if the people create their institutions, then it cannot be that these institutions have shaped the people that make them. The people must possess a kind of unity that precedes the civic identity their decision subsequently creates.

This conundrum—about who or what is the people, about the boundary between those who belong to the people and those who don't—suffuses the constitutions of several postcommunist European countries. The Hungarian constitution presupposes the Hungarian nation, understood as common descent and shared culture; it speaks of "We, the members of the Hungarian nation." Its preamble "recognizes the role of Christianity in preserving nationhood" and praises "our king Saint Stephen" for making Hungary part of "Christian Europe." The preamble goes on to speak of safeguarding "our heritage, our unique language, [and] Hungarian culture" before mentioning the languages and cultures of other nationalities living in Hungary.

The Polish constitution embodies a similar principle but tries to render it less overtly exclusionary: "We the Polish Nation," it begins, "all citizens of the Republic, both those who believe in God as the source of truth, justice, good, and beauty, as well as those not sharing such faith, but respecting those universal values as arising from other sources, equal in rights and obligations towards the common good—Poland, beholden to our ancestors . . . for our culture rooted in the Christian heritage of the nation and in universal human values, recognizing our responsibility before God or our own consciences, Hereby establish this Constitution of the Republic of Poland." The Poles are a people because they agree on fundamental principles, even if they disagree as to the principles' source.

Peoplehood sometimes contains an element of self-creation: we are a separate and distinct people because we say we are and are prepared to defend this claim with our lives. In *Federalist* No. 2, Jay refers to those "who, by their joint counsels, arms, and efforts, fighting side by side throughout a long and bloody war, have nobly established their general liberty and independence."[5] The signers of the Declaration pledged to one another "our lives, our fortunes, and our sacred honor." Through the long and bloody war that followed, they redeemed this pledge and proved to one another that they belonged to a meaningful commonality. Peoplehood was no longer an abstract assertion but a lived reality that colonists who had remained loyal to the British king could not fully share.

Claims based on shared experience, however, are intrinsically limited. Their writ runs out as those who participated in the experience die off. It either morphs into a principle of common descent—the Daughters of the American Revolution—or needs the supplement of some other commonality in which those who come later can participate. Keynoting a DAR convention, FDR reminded the women they were "descended from immigrants." But Housing and Urban Development Secretary Ben Carson got into trouble when he referred to his fellow African Americans in these terms. Our history of slavery means that our shared peoplehood requires something more capacious than the voluntary act of coming to America.

Whatever conception of peoplehood we may endorse, as modern men and women we are apt to believe that there is no alternative to the republican principle. We should set aside this narrow and complacent conviction; there are viable alternatives to the people as sources of legitimacy.

Contemporary autocrats, for example, often claim legitimacy and authorization based on their special insight into the values and desires of their people. Vladimir Putin claims that by promoting social order, traditional values, and the restoration of Russia as a great power, he is doing what the overwhelming majority of Russians want—indeed, what Russians have always wanted. Outside observers may say, with justice, that he rigs elections, manipulates public opinion, and oversees the murder of his political rivals. But the deeper truth, Putin insists, is that his regime rests on his people's conviction that he understands them, an intuitive bond that cuts deeper than more formal systems of public authorization. As Venezuela's Hugo Chávez tacked toward authoritarianism, he increasingly cited a special connection with his people. It is probably not accidental that after his death, his supporters regarded him with quasi-religious reverence.

For adherents of many religions, God is the ultimate basis of government. For religions such as Judaism and Islam, whose revelation takes the form of law, divine authority extends to many details of civic life, and civil law is legitimate only to the extent that it corresponds to God's law. Many Islamists believe that democracy is un-Islamic because it denies the principle on which shari'a rests. Many Orthodox Jews take the position that when civil law and halacha conflict, the former must give way, a principle that can lead believers to violent resistance and even the murder of public officials.

Another alternative to popular sovereignty is meritocracy—the proposition that the power to decide rests on knowledge and skill that some individuals possess in greater measure than others. Meritocrats need not deny the moral equality of human beings, as Brahmins once did, but they do distinguish between moral equality and political equality, which they say rests on the counterfactual claim that political competence is equally distributed among all citizens.

Meritocracy can include—I would say must include—moral as well as cognitive claims. It is not enough for leaders to know how to advance the public welfare; they must also intend it. The ensemble of knowledge, skill, and concern for the common good, say the meritocrats, entitles some individuals to shape forms of government as well as public policy. Government may be for the people without being of or by the people.

These considerations compel us to broaden our understanding of political justification. Legitimate government is determined by looking to the origins of power; good government is determined by looking to the purposes of power. This is the sense in which Aristotle speaks of good and bad regimes: if the ruling authorities, whatever their form and origin, use their privileges to promote justice and the common good, they constitute a good regime.

There is a modern example of this paradigm: the city-state of Singapore. International assessments of government focus on three dimensions. The first is a government's performance in producing the results people want, including rising incomes, health, safety, and security. In this respect, Singapore is near the top. The second involves measures of government effectiveness, regulatory quality, rule of law, and control of corruption. Here again, Singapore stands near the top. The third dimension includes democratic participation and personal liberties. Along this dimension, Singapore ranks in the bottom half.

What are we to make of this disparity? Singapore's longtime strongman Lee Kuan Yew once asserted, "The ultimate test of the value of a political system is whether it helps that society establish conditions that improve the standard of living for the majority of its people."[6] Calvin Cheng, a Singapore-based political observer, added: "Freedom is being able to walk on the streets unmolested in the wee hours in the morning, to be able to leave one's door open and not fear that one would be burgled. Freedom is the woman who can ride buses and trains alone; freedom is not having to avoid certain subway stations after night falls."[7]

Judged against FDR's "Four Freedoms," Singapore is a mixed bag. It ranks very high for freedom from want, slightly less so for freedom from fear. But when it comes to freedom of worship, Singapore's performance is spotty. For example, it bans Jehovah's Witnesses, on the ground that they refuse to salute the flag, pledge allegiance to the state, or serve in the military. The United States Supreme Court once endorsed a similar view but repudiated it in the landmark case of *West Virginia v. Barnette* (1943). And Singapore ranks low on freedom of expression, scoring 51 on the Freedom House 0-to-100 scale, where 0 represents the best performance and 100 the worst.[8] Singapore is perhaps the clearest counterexample to the "modernization theory" hypothesis that as countries become more prosperous, they embrace democracy. As the late Milton Friedman once observed, Singapore demonstrates that it is possible to combine robust market economics with highly authoritarian governance.

Democracy

I can treat the concept of democracy more briefly because Robert Dahl's formulation, which I follow, has become canonical.[9] At the most basic level, democracy requires the equality of all citizens along with a broadly inclusive scope for citizenship. A society in which all citizens are equal but only 10 percent of adults are citizens would not, today, count as a democracy.

Majoritarian rule is the other key pillar of democratic governance. This means, first, that public decisions are made by popular majorities of citizens whose votes all count equally; and, second, that democratic decision-making extends to a maximally wide range of public matters. In Dahl's view, majoritarianism is limited only by the liberties and powers—freedom of speech, assembly, and the press, among others—that citizens need to influence public decisions.

In this conception of democracy unmodified by any adjective, there is nothing essentially undemocratic about majoritarian decisions that systematically go against the interests of specific individuals and groups—as long as their democratic equality, inclusion, and power are not touched. Nor are majoritarian decisions undemocratic if they invade privacy rights. Nor is it undemocratic per se to conduct judicial proceedings in the same manner as legislative affairs. The assembly that condemned Socrates may have been wrong, but it was fully democratic. If it wishes, a democratic public may embrace the maxim that it is better for ten guilty individuals to go free than for one innocent individual to be found guilty, but it is no less democratic if it adopts the opposite view.

Constitutionalism

Constitutionalism denotes basic, enduring structures of formal institutional power, typically but not always codified in writing. This codified structure is "basic" in that it provides the basis for the conduct of public life. And it is "enduring" because it typically involves entrenchment—some mechanism that makes it harder to change the structure than to amend or reverse decisions made within it.

Constitutions rest on some principle (usually explicit) of authorization. In the case of the United States, the people declare their power to authorize the Constitution in its opening words. In Iran, the people are also the ultimate authorizer, but they are the people of a particular religious community: "The Constitution of the Islamic Republic of Iran advances the cultural, social, political, and economic institutions of Iranian society based on Islamic principles and norms, which represent an honest aspiration of the Islamic Ummah." Greece and Ireland combine these principles differently. The Greek constitution claims to speak "in the name of the Holy and Consubstantial and Indivisible Trinity" but goes on to declare: "Popular sovereignty is the foundation of government." The Irish constitution invokes "the name of the Most Holy Trinity, from Whom is all authority" but says also: "We the people of [Ireland] ... do hereby adopt, enact, and give to ourselves this Constitution."

Constitutions typically not only incorporate basic institutions and principles of authorization but also state the purposes of the governments they create. The Preamble to the U.S. Constitution could simply have asserted the basis of its authority: "We the people of the United States do ordain and establish this Constitution for the United States of America." Instead, it interrupts this statement with the words "in order to," after which it declares the ends to which the constitutional order is directed.

Constitutions are double-edged: they both organize power and establish boundaries for the institutions that wield it. These limits can be horizontal, thus the familiar "separation of powers" and "checks and balances." They can also be vertical: through federalism, public power is divided among different levels of jurisdiction.

Even taken together, these limits need not constrain public power in the aggregate. Constitutionalism is compatible with an understanding of public power as total. If the national government has limited police powers while subordinate jurisdictions are free to regulate what the national government may not, then in principle there is nothing beyond government's reach. This is why the decision to limit public power in all its aspects marks the line between constitutionalism per se and the specific type of constitutionalism we call "liberal."

Liberalism

Benjamin Constant famously distinguished between the "liberty of the ancients" and the "liberty of the moderns." For the ancients, liberty consisted in the "active participation in collective power," that is, direct self-government.[10] The transition from cities to states—the size of modern political communities—makes this impossible, even for those founded on republican principles.

Recall President Lincoln's famous formula: government of the people, by the people, and for the people. "Of the people" denotes the republican principle of popular authorization. "For the people" denotes government that acts to preserve liberty and promote the common good. But what about "by the people"? This applies the majoritarian principle to modern republics, but only in the sense that the people choose those who are to represent and govern them. Legislative, executive, and judicial processes are not conducted by the people themselves.

One might conclude, then, that the liberty of the moderns consists in the selection of representatives through free and fair elections in which all may participate on equal terms. But this is only part of the story. In fact, Constant says, the modern alternative to direct participation in government is the "peaceful enjoyment of individual independence."[11] The exclusion of most citizens, most of the time, from direct self-government opens up a large sphere of noncivic life—economic, social, cultural, religious—which citizens expect to conduct on their own terms.

This brings us to the core idea of liberalism—creating a sphere beyond the rightful reach of government in which individuals can enjoy independence and privacy. In this spirit, the Declaration of Independence both invokes and limits the republican principle. Because all human beings are endowed with rights that governments do not create and individuals may not surrender, the republican principle can authorize only forms of government that honor them. Governments are created to "secure these rights," not to redefine or abridge them. It is government's betrayal of this end that warrants public action to change it.

Scope limitations express themselves through negation. The U.S. Constitution says that Congress or the states may not legislate in specific areas. If they do so, the abuse is not so much the content of the law as it is the subject of the law, which extends public power beyond its due bounds.

Putting the Conceptual Pieces Together

We can now venture a more precise characterization of liberal democracy. This type of political order rests on the republican principle, takes constitutional form, and contains all the building blocks of Dahl's democracy. At the same time, it accepts and enforces the liberal principle that the legitimate scope of public power is limited, which involves some abridgement of majoritarianism as the modus operandi of decision-making. A liberal order may use devices such as supermajorities or even unanimity rules to enforce these liberal limits, or deploy constitutional courts insulated from direct public pressure to police the perimeter beyond which even supermajorities may not go.

We can also list principal threats to liberal democracy. They include:

- Straightforward denials of the republican principle
- Exclusionary ethnic, historical, class, or religious conceptions of "the people"
- Claims to legitimacy based on assertions of special insight into the people's hearts and minds
- Religion and meritocracy as substitutes for public authorization
- Extra-constitutional uses of public power in circumstances other than emergencies
- Denials of egalitarian and inclusive conceptions of citizenship
- Attachment of greater weight to some citizens' votes and political rights than others
- Disregard for limits on the legitimate exercise of public power
- International arrangements that restrict a sovereign people's power to make democratic decisions

Theory should not bewitch us, however, into making these matters simpler than they are. Although the Polish constitution invokes religion as a basis of the values that define Polish citizens, it also acknowledges alternative paths to these values. You need not be Catholic to be a good Pole, as long as you can endorse on other grounds the shared understanding that defines and unifies all Poles. Another example: meritocracy is not completely incompatible with liberal democracy. There may be specific sectors, such as the judiciary or the central bank, where special knowledge and expertise are essential qualifications. Liberal democratic stability depends on institutions that can carry out such specialized functions with competence and integrity. But from a liberal democratic perspective, these meritocratic claims must be publicly acknowledged if they are to be legitimate. The people must authorize the institutions that allow meritocracy its rightful place within liberal democracy. It is not illegitimate for the people to change their minds and withdraw the powers that they have conferred on such institutions. Historians debate whether Andrew Jackson was right to block the reauthorization of the Bank of the United States, but they agree that doing so was a legitimate exercise of liberal democratic power.

A third example: the restriction on extra-constitutional activities can become self-defeating if pushed too far. The classic example in the United States is Abraham Lincoln's decision to suspend the writ of habeas corpus at the outset of the Civil War. The constitutional power to do this almost certainly rested with Congress, not the president. Lincoln defended his breach of a specific constitutional provision as necessary to preserve the entire constitutional order. Not even the most hallowed principle of Anglo-American jurisprudence could be permitted to stand in the way of acts needed to save the broader cause of liberal democracy. If Lincoln had had tyrannical ambitions, historians would judge the breach harshly. But he didn't, and they haven't.

Liberal Democracy and the Market Economy

The theoretical categories I have explored thus far leave out a defining feature of contemporary liberal democracies: their commitment to economic growth and prosperity as a central aim of public policy, and to suitably regulated markets as the best way of achieving it. There are good reasons for this commitment. Growth tends to expand the middle class, and larger middle classes often promote the consolidation of liberal democratic institutions. Economic retreat, conversely, puts pressure on these institutions and on the norms that undergird them.

The economic turmoil between the twentieth century's two world wars opened the door to nondemocratic movements and regimes. Sustained economic growth after World War II increased liberal democracy's global credibility. The policies and institutions that far-sighted statesmen put in place enabled Europe and Japan to rise from the ashes of war, embrace democracy, and participate in the greatest period of liberty, broad-based prosperity, and peace in human history. Now the continuing effectiveness of these institutions is in doubt.

The Great Recession shattered complacent assumptions on both sides of the Atlantic. Nearly a decade after the recession began, Europe is still struggling to accelerate economic growth and reduce record unemployment to more normal levels. The recovery in the United States, though sustained, has been slow, and median household incomes barely equal the level reached at the end of the last century. Across the Pacific, two decades of economic stagnation, now exacerbated by demographic decline, have left Japan wondering about the way forward. (Prime Minister Abe's economic renewal program may well represent his country's last chance to avert unending stagnation.) At the same time, the startling rise of China and equally startling success of Singapore offer alternative models of state capitalism decoupled from democratic governance. These developments leave market democracies uncertain of their future.

At first glance, this mood reflects the economic situation rather than broader misgivings about liberal democracy. But the centrality of economic well-being in our politics reflects long-held assumptions about the purposes of our politics. If economic growth and well-being are in jeopardy, so are our political arrangements.

We have known since Aristotle that stable constitutional polities rest on a large, self-confident middle class in an economic order not riven by extremes of wealth and poverty. For Aristotle, these conditions were products of chance and good fortune. In modern times, they have become objectives of economic and social policy.

Economic growth has become more than a material goal; it is a moral enterprise as well. As Benjamin Friedman puts it in his magisterial book *The Moral Consequences of Economic Growth:* "The value of a rising standard of living lies not just in the concrete improvements it brings to how individuals live but in how it shapes the social, political and, ultimately, the moral character of a people. Economic growth—meaning a rising standard of living for the clear majority of citizens—more often than not fosters greater opportunity, tolerance of diversity, social mobility, commitment to fairness, and dedication to democracy . . . Even societies that have already made great advances in these very dimensions, for example, most of today's Western democracies, are more likely to make still further progress when their living standards rise. But when living standards stagnate or decline, most societies make little if any progress toward any of these goals, and in all too many instances they plainly retrogress."[12]

That is why a central question the West now faces is whether the next generation will again achieve broadly shared prosperity or experience stagnant living standards. Prosperity is both the oil that lubricates the machinery of government and the glue that binds society together. Stagnation means a continuation of gridlocked, zero-sum politics and a turn away from the spirit of generosity that only a people confident of its future can sustain.

THREE

The Populist Challenge

The distribution of economic surpluses is the daily business of normal politics in liberal democracies. The process is never free of conflict, but it is usually conducive to compromise. When growth halts, however, and the challenge becomes the allocation of losses in a zero-sum or negative-sum environment, political life is very different. Human experience suggests (and behavioral economists confirm) that the pain of loss exceeds the pleasure of gain. While failing to improve one's well-being is dispiriting, losing ground is bitter.

Other unwelcome changes can exacerbate these difficulties. When immigrants who speak, dress, and worship differently are seen as competing unfairly for scarce jobs and services, they can become the focal point for the ire of longtime residents. When governments fail to respond, they may be seen as indifferent or worse. And when outside forces—international institutions and treaties, among others—are held responsible for impeding effective responses to domestic ills, an upsurge of nationalist sentiment is inevitable.

Some citizens of liberal democracies—typically those with higher levels of education and resources—welcome economic, demographic, and cultural change. Other citizens experience these changes as a threat to established arrangements, or even to social order. Negative sentiments about immigrants, elites, and foreigners are activated and become the linchpins for a narrative of blame. When governments seem unwilling or unable to abate the threat, individuals and groups who feel the threat most acutely search for new leaders who are strong enough to restore order.[1]

The politics of blame provides fertile ground for demagogues who know how to play on people's hopes and fears. Their message is typically some form of populism: the people are virtuous; the elites are corrupt; we should set aside the subtleties of experts and rely on ordinary citizens' common sense.

Demagogues frequently begin by working within the political system, but all too often they and their followers come to regard democratic institutions as part of the problem. When times are hard, different social and economic groups in modern polities struggle with one another, each striving to minimize its losses. Elected governments mirror these divisions, making it hard for them to act effectively. Temporizing and dithering further stoke public discontent.

One consequence is the growth of extremist parties. The far left and populist right have surged while the long-dominant center-left and center-right parties have suffered huge losses. In France, neither the center-left Socialist candidate nor the center-right Republican candidate made it to the final round of the 2017 presidential election. There is a certain rough justice to this, of course; the established parties presided over a decade of stagnation that was bound to end badly.

In the Europe of the 1930s, these phenomena led to contempt for parliamentary democracy and a willingness to embrace nondemocratic alternatives. Prominent intellectuals praised fascism, communism, and Nazism, not least for their capacity to act boldly. Liberal democracy is far more robust today. Still, it is not hard to detect a rising admiration for China's ability to mobilize resources for transformative public investments. The Chinese government can build entire cities faster than U.S. localities can complete an environmental impact study.

Unlike the totalitarian ideologies of the twentieth century, the Chinese model has no roots in Western culture and little resonance as a replacement for liberal democracy, at least in countries with established systems. (The developing world may be more open to it.) The populism now flourishing throughout the West is a different matter. The question is whether it represents only a corrective to unfair and obsolete policies or something more serious—a threat to liberal democracy itself.

Populism Defined

Populism is sometimes regarded less as a distinctive ideology than as an emotion-laden stance. There is something to this belief: populists typically display disappointment at frustrated economic expectation, resentment against rules they regard as rigged and against special interests and wealthy elites who are profiting at their expense, and fear of threats to their physical and cultural security. Combined, these emotions often yield anger, which talented politicians can mobilize in their pursuit of political power.

But to stop at this point would be to leave half the story untold. Unlike the great "isms" of the twentieth century, populism lacks an elaborated theory and canonical texts. It does, however, have a coherent structure. Jan-Werner Müller, a leading scholar of contemporary populism, writes that it "is not anything like a codified doctrine, but it is a set of distinct claims and has what one might call an inner logic."[2]

Populism distinguishes between the "people" and the "elite." Each of these groups is understood as homogeneous: the people have one set of interests and values, the elite another, and they are not only different but fundamentally opposed. The divisions are moral as well as empirical: populism understands the people as uniformly virtuous, the elite as hopelessly corrupt at the people's expense. If the people are homogeneous and virtuous, there is no reason they should not govern themselves and their society without institutional restraints. After all, populist leaders claim, they alone represent the people, the only legitimate force in society. As Cas Mudde puts it, populism claims that "politics should be an expression of the *volonté générale* (general will) of the people."[3]

Placed against the previous chapter's conceptual template, populism accepts the principles of popular sovereignty and democracy, understood straightforwardly as the exercise of majoritarian power, but is skeptical about constitutionalism to the extent that formal, bounded institutions and structures impede majorities from working their will. It takes an even dimmer view of liberal protections for individuals and minority groups.[4]

It might seem, then, that contemporary populism is what many scholars and at least one national leader call "illiberal democracy" —a governing system capable of translating popular preferences into public policy without the impediments that have prevented liberal democracies from responding effectively to urgent problems. From this perspective, populism is a threat not to democracy per se but rather to the dominant liberal variant of democracy that has now been rendered obsolete.

Mudde argues that "although the populist radical right is not antidemocratic in a procedural sense . . . core tenets of its ideology stand in fundamental tension with *liberal* democracy." In fact, he contends, the populist critique of liberal democracy as now practiced is not without merit: it represents "an illiberal democratic response to undemocratic liberalism."[5] When elites take important issues such as economic, monetary, and regulatory policies off the public agenda and assign them to institutions insulated from public scrutiny and influence, they invite precisely the popular revolt that now threatens to overwhelm them. From this perspective, populism is less an attack on democracy than a response to a deficit of democracy.

But matters are not so simple. Because populism embraces the republican principle of popular sovereignty, it faces the question inherent in this principle: Who are the people? Historically, right-leaning populists have emphasized shared ethnicity and common descent, while left-leaning populists have often defined the people in class terms, excluding those with wealth and power. Recently, a third definition has entered public debate—the people versus cultural elites. "Real people" eat hamburgers, listen to country and western music, and watch *Duck Dynasty;* globalist snobs do whatever PBS, NPR, and the *New York Times* deem refined.

Speaking at a campaign rally in May 2016, candidate Donald Trump offered an off-the-cuff example of this thesis. "The only important thing is the unification of the people," he declared, because "the other people don't mean anything."[6] There we have it: the people (that is, the real people) against the other people who are somehow outside and alien.

This approach raises some obvious difficulties. First, it is divisive by definition. Within the context of popular sovereignty, dividing a country's population into the people and the others suggests that some parts of the population are not really part of the people and do not deserve to share in self-government. Individuals outside the charmed circle of the people may therefore be excluded from equal citizenship, violating the principle of inclusion that is part of Dahl's definition of democracy.

Here is a second difficulty: the populist definition of the people is inherently counterfactual. Says Müller, populists "speak and act *as if* the people could develop a singular judgment, a singular will, and hence a singular, unambiguous mandate."[7] But of course they cannot. In circumstances of even partial liberty, different social groups will have different interests, values, and origins. Plurality, not homogeneity, characterizes most peoples most of the time. Imposing the assumption of uniformity on the reality of diversity not only distorts the facts but also elevates the characteristics of some social groups over others. To the extent that this occurs, populism becomes a threat to democracy, because "democracy requires pluralism and the recognition that we need to find fair terms of living together as free, equal, but also irreducibly diverse citizens."[8] Whatever may have been possible in classical republics, no form of identity politics can serve as the basis for a modern democratic society.

Equally counterfactual is the proposition that the people are uniformly virtuous. We are not, individually or collectively. Political movements based on this premise inevitably come to grief, but not before disappointment gives way to a violent search for hidden enemies. (Recall Robespierre's "Republic of Virtue.")

When paired with the assumed corruption of elites, the presumption of the people's virtue undermines democratic practice. Decision-making in circumstances of diversity typically requires compromise, but compromise is hard to accept if one group or party believes that the other embodies evil. How can it be good to compromise with them? Better no action than dishonorable concessions to the forces of darkness. (In circumstances of deep partisan polarization, of course, harshly negative judgments of the opposing party and its supporters are not confined to a single party or political tendency.)

Circumstances like these lead Müller and others to express impatience with scholarly defenders of populism. It is certainly true, he writes, that "populism can never be combined with liberalism, if one means by the latter something like a respect for pluralism and an understanding of democracy as necessarily involving checks and balances (and, in general, constraints on the popular will)." But there is a broader problem: "What follows from [an] understanding of populism as an exclusionary form of identity politics is that populism tends to pose a danger to democracy." For this reason, "we should stop the thoughtless invocation of 'illiberal democracy.' Populists damage democracy as such, and the fact that they have won elections does not give their projects automatic democratic legitimacy."[9]

International relations scholars Jeff Colgan and Robert Keohane offer an account of populism that includes but goes beyond a purportedly homogeneous and virtuous people. Populists believe that the people are locked in battle with hostile domestic elites and foreign forces. Countering these adversaries requires strong leaders unencumbered by countermajoritarian institutions. It requires, as well, the unflinching reassertion of national sovereignty against international arrangements that limit the people's ability to determine its own destiny. In different contexts, this can mean anything from British Leavers' antipathy to the European Union to Donald Trump's skepticism about the value of alliances.[10]

The Dispute

While definitions clarify our thinking, they cannot resolve the dispute over how great a threat populism poses to liberal democracy. We must turn to the facts on the ground, where one-size-fits-all theories cannot be applied effectively to every situation. The British electorate's decision to leave the European Union was a populist uprising against elites in both political parties, partly driven by anti-immigrant sentiment. But this vote, which reconfigured British politics and could lead to a break with Scotland, does not really threaten liberal democracy in the United Kingdom. At the other end of the spectrum, there is reason to fear that Hungary's populist shift could end in an outright breach of democratic norms and institutions. The European Union is expressing similar fears about the Polish government's effort to curb the independence of the country's judiciary.

The United States is a disputed intermediate case. But before I take up that subject, I turn to Continental Europe, where three countries—Hungary, Poland, and France—face challenges from populist movements whose political trajectory could have Continental or even global consequences.

FOUR

The European Project and Its Enemies

The devastation wrought by World War II gave way to a bold quest
for European federalism, Continent-wide socioeconomic security,
and military and diplomatic peace among nation-states. The architects working to build a "United States of Europe" found a home
for their ambitious political vision in efforts toward greater economic cooperation. The European Union began as the European
Coal and Steel Community, in which participating member nations
pooled coal and steel production in hopes that closer economic ties
would make war between European powers less likely. For many
fans of the European project, the creation of a single currency
marked one of the greatest steps toward "ever-closer union."

While technocrats worked to build a European polity, supranational citizenship elicited only weak enthusiasm from voters.
Dampening celebrations of the Union's birth, national referenda
on the 1992 Maastricht Treaty establishing the European Union
drew low voter turnout, narrow margins of victory, and the recognition of member state exemptions.

The Eurozone financial crisis, which began in 2009, was the ultimate test of public faith. As member states struggled with sovereign debt, negotiated bailout packages, and implemented austerity measures, voters throughout Europe blamed the regulatory framework designed by bureaucratic elites for weakened social protections and slow economic recovery. In the wake of the crisis, formerly marginal populist parties began to enjoy unprecedented electoral success, and new parties entered the scene with fervent support.

In Denmark, Sweden, Finland, and Norway, parts of the electorate embraced welfare tribalism, defending ethnic natives as the exclusive beneficiaries of Nordic social democracy and castigating Muslims, immigrants, and asylum seekers as drains on the public fisc. In 2017, Austrian voters gave the anti-immigrant Freedom Party 26 percent of the vote, up from 21 percent in 2013. The center-right People's Party won by adopting much of the FP's agenda.

Political parties led by charismatic leaders, including self-proclaimed Marxists, have made significant gains in southern European countries that have experienced some of the most suffocating austerity measures. In Greece, Syriza's Alexis Tsipras is now the prime minister. In Spain, Pablo Iglesias's Podemos gained sixty-nine seats in the Spanish parliament in a single election. Beppe Grillo's Five Star Movement in Italy, founded in 2009, received more than 25 percent of the vote in 2013, securing more than a hundred seats in the Chamber of Deputies. Although far-left politician Jean-Luc Mélenchon did not make it past the first round of the 2017 French presidential election, he enjoyed three times the support of the Socialist Party's candidate.

Despite its long history of Euroskepticism, the United Kingdom stunned the world with its vote in the summer of 2016 to leave the European Union. Even in Germany—a country where many believed historical guilt would create an eternal aversion to populism—the anti-immigrant Alternative for Germany received nearly 13 percent of the popular vote in the 2017 general election and entered the Bundestag. Hungary, Poland, and France offer the three leading cases of contemporary European populism. Prime Minister Viktor Orban's pledge to turn Hungary into an "illiberal democracy," the efforts of the Law and Justice Party's Kaczynski twins to reject Poland's postcommunist transition and create a "Fourth Republic," and the National Front's promise to wrest control from an oligarchic and globalist elite demonstrate what contemporary populist politics looks like. Hungary and Poland show what can happen when populists gain control.

While every country's populism demands a careful assessment of its unique causes and consequences, each of these cases can be understood as part of a collective European story. Pope Francis's recent speech on the European Union's sixtieth birthday reflected the growing divide between the political orientation of European elites and common populist refrains. Speaking to the heads of state and government leaders of the bloc, Francis declared: "Politics needs [the] kind of leadership which avoids appealing to emotions."[1] But Mabel Berezin, an expert on the European far right, notes that in legitimizing fear, right-wing politicians prove they "are often more adept than their liberal counterparts at valorizing emotion and responding viscerally to events."[2] Populists, in other words, provide a collective political voice for feelings of vulnerability. As Berezin observes, in the wake of terrorist attacks it is not hard to see why the common line urging voters not to give in to a fear that "lets the terrorists win" often loses out to a populist message that validates fear and energizes the quest for strong, protective leadership.

In his speech, Francis also called for "a spirit of solidarity" to "[devise] policies that can make the union as a whole develop harmoniously." But European solidarity holds little appeal for voters who see the bloc as a threat to their economic well-being and sense of cultural belonging. Instead, the calls for solidarity uttered by populists today are anti-European; one slogan on Marine Le Pen's website reads, "Solidarity with the victims of fiscal injustice and eurosterity!" Francis insisted that "Europe finds new hope when she refuses to yield to fear or close herself off in false forms of security." But for many voters, the European project itself represents a failed security strategy. In this environment, fearful voters are drawn to older forms of national self-protection.[3]

The European project now confronts populists who challenge liberal democracy's capacity to satisfy rank-and-file citizens. While proponents of Europeanization make idealistic appeals to Continent-wide political and economic solidarity, populists offer an unabashed nationalism that guarantees security against economic dislocation, terrorism, and threats to individual and cultural identity. It is not difficult to see why populists throughout Europe are making headway against long-established parties and institutions.

Unlike the authoritarian and totalitarian movements of the interwar period, today's populists do not mount a frontal attack on democracy itself. Instead, as Müller argues, the threat to democracy comes "from within the democratic world—the political actors posing the danger speak the language of democratic values."[4] Populism represents a reaction—to some extent a corrective—to an elite-driven project that proceeded over the heads of many citizens. Still, populists' rejection of pluralist politics challenges the liberal democratic order, which stands or falls with the recognition of individual rights, social diversity, and the need for reasonable compromise among competing interests.

Populism in Hungary and Poland

After the fall of the Berlin Wall in 1989, Hungary and Poland underwent remarkably successful and rapid transitions to democratic governance and market liberalization. Fears that these postcommunist states would be gripped by authoritarianism, nationalism, and xenophobia were allayed by widespread support for liberal norms and consistent moves toward alignment with the West. Today, however, populist and illiberal political forces in both countries are threatening to usher in a new era of democratic backsliding. Hungary's Fidesz and Poland's Law and Justice openly embrace authoritarian actions, delegitimize political opposition, call for extreme majoritarianism, and are skeptical of or openly hostile to the rights of powerless minorities.

For many proponents of liberal democracy, the postcommunist transition signaled that the West had decisively won the ideological battles of the twentieth century. It was conventional wisdom that democratic consolidation marked a permanent turn to liberal democracy. Hungary and Poland held their first free parliamentary elections in 1990 and 1991, respectively. They joined NATO in 1999, and in 2004 they became members of the European Union along with eight other countries. Throughout the 1990s, Hungary benefited from an influx of foreign investment, while Poland was heralded as the poster child for market-friendly reform. By 2014, the Polish economy had grown more than 4 percent a year for two decades, making it the sixth-largest economy in the European Union and the Continent's fastest growing. The Polish standard of living more than doubled between 1989 and 2012. Against this backdrop, the electoral success of these countries' populist movements has sent shockwaves across Europe.[5]

A closer look helps explain why democracy is challenged in Hungary and Poland. Despite impressive aggregate gains, many felt excluded from the economic growth that accompanied market liberalization. In Hungary, the 1990s and early 2000s saw growing socioeconomic and urban-rural divisions affecting the life prospects of Hungarians. During Hungary's postcommunist transition, inflation rose while real wages declined. Although Poland's overall economy improved significantly in the postcommunist era, rural Poland stagnated, and large-scale structural unemployment forced many Poles to seek work abroad. In some areas of the rural east, where Law and Justice enjoys significant support, unemployment is double the national average. As a trade union activist from eastern Poland remarked, "This is the backwater of Europe. If it could, Warsaw would fill it with forest."[6]

In both Hungary and Poland, populist parties have capitalized on these widespread economic woes. Originally founded as a student movement in 1988, Hungary's Fidesz has undergone several changes, including ideological flirtations with libertarianism and conservatism. Since 2010, when it won a supermajority in the Hungarian parliamentary elections, the party has settled on a firmly nationalist stance. Fidesz's electoral success followed revelations that Hungary's Socialist prime minister lied about the country's collapsing budget to secure his reelection, a scandal many connect with Hungary's 2008 bailout and ensuing austerity measures. It is no surprise, then, that Fidesz's antibank rhetoric, staunch opposition to foreign investors, and attack on multinational financial institutions resonated with voters in the 2010 election.

But Fidesz does not merely propose an alternative to the European Union's globalist outlook. The party combines its promise to bring economic prosperity with calls for an emboldened Christian-national culture. In a recent address to the European People's Party Congress, Orban decried the immigration of Muslims into Europe and called upon the party to protect Christian identity, national pride, and traditional family values. These declarations underscore Orban's anti-pluralist aims.[7] As Müller notes, "For Orban, Christianity is irrelevant as a guide to individual action. What matters is Christendom as a collective identity that helps to demarcate good Europeans from bad Muslims."[8]

In a similar vein, Poland's Law and Justice Party promotes economic populism and calls for a "Christian democracy." After winning 27 percent of the vote in the 2005 parliamentary election, the party failed to hold the presidency or substantial parliamentary representation for several years. In 2015, however, it won 38 percent of the vote and retook control of the government. Campaigning on a traditionalist critique of post-Soviet Poland as corrupt and in need of moral and political renewal, the party called for regulation and intervention in the market to lift up Polish citizens. These demands included an increase in the minimum wage, improved family benefits, taxation of foreign banks' assets, job creation, and limits on central bank independence.

The Hungarian and Polish populist parties' hostility toward refugees reflects an agenda that is at once economic and cultural. In both countries, about four in ten citizens hold negative views of growing diversity, and majorities believe their society is better off when composed of people from the same nationality, religion, and culture. Hungary surpasses other E.U. member states in its citizens' fervent belief that refugees are a burden, take away jobs and social benefits, and increase the likelihood of terrorism. More than half of Poles advocate refusing refugees entry, even if it comes at the cost of E.U. membership.[9] In this climate, Fidesz and Law and Justice argue that the refugee crisis poses one of the greatest threats to Europe, and the two joined forces in a lawsuit against the European Union's refugee quota system. Jaroslaw Kaczynski, the cofounder (with his brother) of Law and Justice, once warned that the refugees were "bringing in all kinds of parasites" and claimed that Muslim migrants pose a threat to Polish values. Fidesz's Orban declared, "Migration is not a solution but a problem . . . not medicine but a poison. We don't need it and won't swallow it."[10]

The Hungarian government recently introduced a new asylum procedure that places applicants as well as asylum seekers already living in the country in detention camps, and it barred journalists from entering the camps to report on the conditions detainees face. Poland has since proposed the same policy, and this draconian approach has gained support among most European nations whose borders expose them to large refugee flows.

While this situation has brought to light the bleak injustices confronting migrants in Hungary and Poland, the inadequate response from the European Union has revealed how ill-equipped the supranational structure is to confront the populist members within its own ranks. As Elizabeth Collett, the founding director of Migration Policy Institute Europe, recently noted, "For a set of member states increasingly aware of the security of their own borders and the success of nationalist political narratives . . . additional pooling of sovereignty across the EU . . . may prove too much to contemplate. In this scenario, Poland and Hungary may well just be waiting for the rest of the EU to come around to their way of thinking."[11] Facing few consequences, the harsh nationalist approach to refugee management carried out in Hungary and Poland has gained a significant degree of credibility.

Since coming to power, both Fidesz and Law and Justice have restricted the independence of the courts, prohibited the media from reporting in ways that violate "the interests of the nation," and discredited NGOs as "foreign agents." In its first twenty months of governing, Fidesz enacted 365 laws and legal amendments.[12] This wide array of changes included the criminalization of homelessness, media regulations that permit the government to fine media outlets for "imbalanced" or "insulting" coverage, measures that allow ethnic Hungarians living outside the country to vote in national elections, and new restrictions on access to public information. Orban also appointed party insiders to nonpartisan bureaucratic positions, a move that radically transformed the Hungarian civil service. After years of attacking the George Soros–funded Central European

University, Orban's party passed higher education reforms aimed at forcing the school to close its doors.

In Poland, Law and Justice brought its chief prosecutor under the minister of justice, eliminating the position's independence, and licensed the Ministry of the Treasury to appoint the head of public broadcasting. The party has challenged the right of peaceful assembly by enacting a bill that imposes stringent requirements on groups planning public gatherings. It remains to be seen whether the surprising veto by President Andrzej Duda of two bills that would curb the independence of Poland's Constitutional Court will restrain his party's push for ever-greater power over all state and civic institutions.

Here too, the European Union's response has appeared weak. In an effort to thwart further attempts to limit the independence of the judiciary in Poland, the European Commission threatened to trigger Article 7, which would impose sanctions on Poland and suspend the member state's E.U. voting rights. As many have noted, however, the threat lacks credibility: invoking Article 7 would require unanimity among European Council members, including Orban, who has vehemently opposed such actions against Poland. An inability to meaningfully carry out any kind of response at the supranational level to date has proved disheartening. Reacting to the Polish constitutional crisis, a famous Polish dissident noted that "the EU's decision-making system . . . guarantees impunity for populists."[13]

In a famous 2014 speech in which he laid out his vision for Hungary, Orban declared: "The new state that we are building is an illiberal state." Although he and his supporters insist that illiberalism is not a front for autocracy, many observers judge that his vision pays only lip service to democratic ideals. Nevertheless, the strategy on which his populism depends includes the employment of pro-democratic language to legitimate his attack on liberal institutions and practices as antithetical to Hungarian interests. Whether a slide into authoritarianism is the inevitable casualty of building an illiberal state remains to be seen.[14]

However, his rejection of social and political pluralism, explicit when Orban invokes the homogeneity of the people, poses an unambiguous threat to liberal values that could sharpen the party's authoritarian edge. Addressing a group of Fidesz party activists in 2009, Orban declared that "Hungarian politics over the next fifteen to twenty years will not be determined by a dual power bloc, which, due to constant debate regarding values, generates divisive, petty, and unnecessary social consequences. Instead, a large governing party is being formed, a central political field of force, which will be able to address national issues—and this will not be done by constant debates, but it will represent them in its own natural way."[15]

Orban similarly stressed the inefficiencies of multiparty politics in refusing to participate in the debates leading up to the 2010 and 2014 elections: "No policy-specific debates are needed now, the alternatives in front of us are obvious." Law and Justice's Jaroslaw Kaczynski has also described pluralist politics as plagued with "chaos and perpetual war," and the head of Law and Justice's parliamentary caucus, when asked about the need for political compromise, replied, "What kind of compromise do you mean? . . . There's no need for one."[16]

In an effort to delegitimize its political opposition, Law and Justice even performed an "audit" of its predecessor, the centrist, pro-European Civic Platform. This process featured accusations that Civic Platform had wasted billions of government dollars, "sold out" Polish interests to the European Union, and conspired with Russia. For populists, governing in the interests of "the people" and establishing an illiberal state are inextricably linked, because they insist that the people form a homogeneous group whose only disputes are with the elites.

It was only twenty-nine years ago that Poland set out to secure economic and political freedom through liberal democracy. The trade union movement Solidarity, whose success led to Poland's first free elections, organized under the slogan "There is no bread without freedom." As a student dissident in Hungary, Viktor Orban made similar appeals. So what underlies the rejection of liberal democracy in favor of populism with its authoritarian tendencies?

Some argue that the unique structural and historical challenges liberal democracy confronts in postcommunist Eastern Europe strengthen the populist backlash. In Hungary and Poland, they observe, democratic institutions and practices are relatively weak, and civil society remains underdeveloped. In postcommunist countries, moreover, the desire to assert a strong national identity can be explained historically. As John Shattuck notes, "Eastern Europeans were ruled for centuries by successive empires of Ottoman, Russian, Habsburg, fascist, and communist authoritarian regimes. A hunger for national identity and honor among the peoples of the region grew out of oppression by their rulers."[17] Thus, the political climate in Hungary and Poland was ripe for the nativist appeals of populist parties.

Taking a different tack, Ivan Krastev insists that the historic weakness of liberal democracy cannot adequately explain the success of Hungary's and Poland's populist movements. Those seeking to make sense of the rise of populism in Eastern Europe often begin by asking the wrong question: "What is going wrong with postcommunist democracy?" They should focus instead, Krastev argues, on the basic nature of the postcommunist period.

Liberal democracy challenges its citizens in a fundamental way: it asks the powerful to resist majoritarian temptations to safeguard the rights of powerless minorities. Against the immediate historical backdrop of communist oppression, a typical citizen in postcommunist Europe was capable of embracing the more arduous elements of civic participation in liberal democracy. As Krastev writes, "Having seen real state repression, this voter was ready to 'think like a minority' even when in the majority. Communism's role in shaping the self-restraint of this voter was communism's unintentional gift to the cause of liberal-democratic consolidation."[18]

While the postcommunist period accounts for the rapid and successful consolidation of liberal democracy in Eastern Europe, Krastev continues, it also clarifies today's populist challenge. The process of European integration pursued by postcommunist states meant that major economic decisions were removed from the electoral arena, leaving identity politics as a dominant vehicle for political appeals. Polish sociologist and political scientist Rafal Pankowski notes that there was not only economic exclusion, "there was also cultural dislocation and confusion about social values. In the absence of a progressive alternative, social anger came to be channeled through radical identity discourse."[19] This weakness of the liberal democratic transition in combination with the historical fear of multiculturalism in Eastern Europe proved potent. As Krastev writes, "The postcommunist countries know not only the advantages but the dark sides of multiculturalism. . . . For many of them, a return to ethnic diversity suggests a return to the troubled interwar period." This historical context helps clarify today's demographic panic in response to the refugee crisis.[20]

The wave of liberal democratic consolidation after the collapse of the Soviet Union reflected exceptional historical circumstances. When the disease was tyranny, liberal democracy was the cure. But when concrete economic and social issues moved to the fore, the capacity of liberal democratic government to address them became crucial. Populism represents a response to these governments' perceived inability to do so in a genuinely inclusive manner. The groups that felt left behind by economic modernization and cultural liberalism insisted on being heard, and the populist parties responded. As the Hungarian philosopher Ágnes Heller suggests, "We will now see if liberal democracy was only a kind of surface phenomenon, which flourished due to a period of prosperity."[21]

Today, Kaczynski and Orban do not merely promise to enshrine an ethnocentric conception of national identity into public life and laws; they also frame illiberalism as a pragmatic path toward economic prosperity. Orban, laying out his vision for an illiberal democracy, stated, "We are searching for and we are doing our best to find—parting ways with Western European dogmas, making ourselves independent from them—the form of organizing a community, that is capable of making us competitive in this great world-race." Similarly, Kaczynski insists, "It is completely untrue that to achieve western levels of development, we have to adopt their social models. That is hogwash."[22]

France's National Front

In 1972, Jean-Marie Le Pen and a cohort of far-right nationalists founded France's National Front party (the FN) as a political home for military veterans and imperialists frustrated by the loss of France's last major colonial holding in the Algerian war. From its inception, the FN focused on the issue of immigration, attributing French economic woes to the influx of newcomers. Hence the party's slogan: "One million jobless are one million immigrants too many." The party enjoyed its first electoral success in the 1980s when Le Pen received 14 percent of the vote in the first round of the presidential election. In 2002, he shocked many by making it to the second round.

In an effort to "normalize" the party and distance it from its anti-Semitic reputation—Jean-Marie Le Pen infamously referred to the Holocaust gas chambers as a "detail of history"—Marine Le Pen took over her father's post as party president. She maintained many of the party's anti-immigrant and nationalist features but began tailoring its platform to the interests of its rapidly expanding working-class base.

In the 1980s and 1990s, despite mounting economic problems—slow growth, high unemployment, crime, and immigration—many center-left politicians who had staunchly fought on behalf of the working class began accommodating business interests. (A similar process occurred in the United States, the United Kingdom, and Germany.) This strategic choice, in conjunction with a rightward shift in public opinion on issues such as law and order, immigration, and French identity, allowed the FN to tap into working-class discontent.

Although FN supporters place themselves toward the right end of the political spectrum, they are less enthusiastic about a conservative ideology of limited government and more attracted to protection against the uncertainties of a globalizing world. To this end, Marine Le Pen has promised to safeguard French culture from the creeping influence of Islam, the working class from the dominance of financial interests, and the French social model from the drain of undeserving immigrants.

The FN under her leadership has broken its previous electoral records, shaking the French political establishment by winning 27 percent of the vote in both the first and second rounds of the 2015 regional elections. In launching her 2017 presidential campaign, Le Pen declared the FN a movement to reclaim France's "national interest" and to strengthen "the people against the oligarchies."[23] Like her father fifteen years earlier, she made it to the final round of the presidential election, where she received more than one-third of the popular vote.

The National Front wages its fight in the interest of "the people" against three enemies—Islam, globalism, and the French political establishment. The party has taken the lead in defining these threats and enumerating a firm response to them in ways that are especially compelling for those who feel economically vulnerable and culturally threatened. The FN portrays Islam as an attack on French identity, globalism as an attack on French economic prosperity and its social model, and the political establishment an attack on French democracy. Understanding how the FN promises to ameliorate these threats reveals a distinct set of populist challenges to liberal democracy.

France is home to nearly five million Muslims—7.5 percent of its population, one of the highest shares in Europe. This helps explain the National Front's assertion that not just Islamist extremism but Islam itself poses a threat to French security and identity. On the campaign trail, Le Pen claimed that 100 percent of the meat sold around Paris was halal and compared street prayers to Nazi occupation.[24] Her rhetoric validates those inclined to see little difference between the increasing visibility of everyday Muslim practices and the threat of terrorism.

Le Pen does not wage the fight against extremism on religious grounds. Instead, she claims she is preserving French republican values and the secularist doctrine of *laïcité*. As she declares, "Islam is hardly soluble in secularism." Aurelien Mondon, an expert on the French far right, observes that unlike the racists of previous generations, Le Pen invokes a "new kind of racism" that "[does] not rely on 'biological heredity, but [on] the irreducibility of cultural differences.'" This framework resonates with many voters, 63 percent of whom believe that Islam is incompatible with French values.[25]

In an era of routine terrorist attacks in France, the National Front has exploited a growing climate of fear. In a recent survey, 82 percent of French respondents believed another terrorist attack is probable or highly probable.[26] Following the attacks on the Bataclan concert hall, Le Pen demanded the shutdown of immigration into France, called for strengthened military and police forces, pushed for a ban on Islamist organizations and radical mosques, and criticized French president François Hollande for failing to declare a "fight against Islamism." The attack brought the FN a significant surge in public support.

By stoking national security anxieties, the FN taps into the growing climate of fear and asserts itself as the party most capable of a enacting a strong response to imminent national threats.[27] For the FN, Russia is not one of these threats. On the contrary, it is in France's interest to set aside obsolete Cold War habits and maximize cooperation with Vladimir Putin's Russia. Against this backdrop, it is not surprising that Russian-backed hackers penetrated French television networks as purported members of ISIS in an effort to encourage scared French voters to support the National Front in the 2015 regional elections. It is also not surprising that Marine Le Pen received a warm welcome in Moscow just months before the presidential contest.[28]

While terrorist acts generate legitimate worries and require a firm response, populists gain by exaggerating the danger. The risk is that overwrought public fear can lead to hasty, ill-considered reactions that violate the rights of individuals and minority groups with no appreciable gain in safety and security. The U.S. internment of Japanese Americans at the outset of World War II suffices to show that this risk is more than hypothetical.

Globalism, the second enemy identified by the National Front, can be broken down into two elements—transnational capitalism and multiculturalism—which the party presents as affronts to democratic representation and the French social model. According to the National Front, the constraining fiscal criteria of the Eurozone and the European Union's open-borders policy enabling the flow of immigration into France represent zero-sum relationships for the French working class. For the FN, the only adequate response is a "France for the French" strategy that ends the provision of social protections to nonnatives.

As the French left turned away from its traditional working-class constituency to embrace business interests and the political establishment failed to address economic stagnation and chronic unemployment, the FN became a more attractive choice for workers and the unemployed. Its critique of transnational capitalism insists that big-money interests in league with supranational institutions are responsible for France's loss of control over its own economic life. The party castigates nonelected institutions that impose austerity and fiscal discipline, labeling present economic arrangements a "dictatorship of finance and banks" that controls the French government.[29]

With the FN as the new political home for globalization's losers, Le Pen presents her constituency with a cogent message that explains their feelings of vulnerability: Europeanization forces France to concede French economic governance to foreign financial interests, while globalization opens France's borders to an influx of foreign labor. As Cecile Alduy notes, Le Pen provides "a narrative to frame [the] experience of identity loss and downward social mobility." This diagnosis works especially well at a time when most people in France believe globalization threatens the country and hope to win back control from the European Union—without undermining it altogether. Le Pen's policies include promises to reindustrialize France, nationalize commercial banks, and increase the generosity of the French social safety net. By tying economic grievances to the breakdown of fair democratic representation and the promise of self-government, says Alduy, "Le Pen has recast herself as the only leader eager to defend the people's rights, especially the right to self-determination." She vowed that if elected president, she would hold a referendum on France's membership in the European Union.[30]

The FN's pro-worker agenda and promise to take bold action to turn the French economy around are tied to a backlash against the second feature of globalism—multiculturalism. Cas Mudde contends that "the economic program is a secondary feature in the ideologies of populist radical right parties. . . . Most of the time, [these] parties use their economic program to put into practice their core ideological positions (nativism, authoritarianism, and populism) and to expand their electorate." Whether or not this is true as a general proposition, the evidence suggests FN supporters are united less by a shared economic agenda than by a shared animus against immigrants. The party's support is strongest in the Northeast and Southeast, where a 2013 opinion poll found that more than 90 percent of voters in both regions believe France has too many immigrants. The two regions, however, disagree over issues of taxation. A majority of FN voters in the Southeast believe taxes on the rich are too high, whereas 42 percent of FN voters in the Northeast believe they are not high enough.[31]

By bringing together voters with divergent attitudes on economic policy, the FN increased its influence in the political mainstream. Also helpful were more traditional conservative politicians like Nicolas Sarkozy, who sought to appeal to the FN's base by lifting long-standing taboos on political discourse. In the case of the FN's anti-immigrant message, Alduy notes, "The topic has become such a land mine that challenging these views is political suicide: left or right, few have the courage to contest with hard facts the National Front's narrative of immigrants stealing jobs and benefits."[32] Giving credence to FN views has become a political necessity.

Mabel Berezin calls the FN's many electoral defeats "fraught with paradox" because these losses came while the FN's issues were becoming "increasingly French issues." In a critical campaign speech, Sarkozy demonstrated how successfully the FN had infiltrated mainstream rhetoric when he declared he was "national without being nationalist" and "of the people without being populist." On the night of his defeat in the first round of the 2007 presidential election, Jean-Marie Le Pen declared, "We have won the battle of ideas: nation and patriotism, immigration and insecurity were put at the heart of the campaign of my adversaries who spread these ideas with a wry pout." Populists don't just win at the ballot box; they also win by changing the political conversation.[33]

On several issues, the FN has opened policy options by putting new ideas on the table. From this standpoint, it could be regarded as a corrective to a center-left/center-right duopoly over political discourse. On the other hand, the dominance of the far right's interpretation of these issues presents a standing challenge to pluralist politics.

The third enemy of French populism is the French political class, which it sees as having failed to ameliorate economic stagnation. The FN has responded to this enemy by breaking down traditional right-left political divisions. As Laurent Bouvet, a French political theorist, observes, "When she pretends to defend the Republic, *laïcité*, women or gay rights, [Marine Le Pen] blurs the traditional image of the far right. . . . She has the political acumen to situate herself right in the center of the political debate by showing that others' solutions don't work and that she can borrow from the repertoire of all political forces—that she is pragmatic but knows where she's heading at the same time."[34]

By drawing from the playbooks of both the right and the left, Le Pen demonstrates to her voters that ideological commitments only create barriers to political efficacy. This strategy of defying right-left politics in the name of pragmatism has worked especially well at a time when French voters are politically disillusioned. Increasing numbers of them are opting to abstain from voting, a mere 23 percent report they trust Parliament, and only 8 percent say they trust established political parties.[35]

It is no surprise that the moderate right began to see potential for electoral gains by courting FN voters. As early as 1986, it began incorporating extreme-right positions into its official program. This process of normalization helped the FN move from the fringe to being a party like any other. The proportion of French people who see the party as a threat to democracy fell from 70 percent in the early 2000s to 47 percent in 2013. It is probably lower today.[36]

The FN's antisystem stance allows the party to flout the political norms that constrain others. Le Pen is able to leverage widespread discontent about the FN's underrepresentation in the French parliament, the undemocratic nature of supranational institutions, and the erosion of faith in French democracy to explain away attacks on her integrity. Responding to accusations that she spent €300,000 in European Parliament funds to pay National Front party staff not employed by the chamber, Le Pen told reporters she refused to pay back the misused money: "I will not submit to the persecution, a unilateral decision taken by political opponents." As one National Front supporter stated, she "is accused of using money for political ends, which is exactly what it's there for. . . . We don't see the point of the European Parliament to begin with." A former member of the Socialist Party who has since become a prominent National Front figure noted, "If Marine is placed under formal investigation, . . . the voters will see it as one more sign of the system being against Marine." The enforcement of liberal democratic standards against populists is thus transmuted into evidence that the political system is against the interests of the people.[37]

As the centrist, pro-European Emmanuel Macron demonstrated, it was possible to run a pragmatic, beyond-left-and-right campaign without appealing to public antipathies—and to prevail on the basis of hope rather than fear. Nonetheless, the far right achieved unprecedented support in this past election. Additionally, roughly half of French voters opted for the far-left and the far-right candidate in the first round of voting, a fact that illustrates the widespread discontent with the French political system. While the victory of Macron offers respite, it does not reveal a broad mandate for his centrist platform. Of those who voted in the second round, 43 percent told survey researchers they supported Macron in an effort to prevent Le Pen from winning, and 33 percent said they voted for him in the hope of political renewal, compared to only 16 percent who cited his program.[38]

The stakes for Europe's future appear high, and the prospect of future populist gains remains. If Macron is able to seize the moment and renew France's sclerotic economy, he will deal a blow to populism by demonstrating that a pragmatic politics of the center can be effective without dividing society and demonizing adversaries. If he fails, the FN remains ready to capitalize on the continuing grievances of many French citizens.

From the European Community to the "Imagined Community"

The architects of European liberal democracy believed that if they built the structure for cooperation between nation-states, a political community would develop naturally. Deepening economic and social integration would lead citizens of member countries to abandon nationalist loyalties and adopt a shared European identity. Today, however, the European Union suffers from a legitimacy crisis, and the anticipated European political community remains a far-off vision.

The European reaction to integration is anything but homogeneous. Younger, well-educated, wealthy, and financially secure citizens are more likely to identify as European, while those who are older, less educated, poorer, and financially struggling are more likely to retain national identities and embrace Euroskepticism. While majorities in Hungary and Poland believe that European Union membership benefits their country, approval of the Union drops among those experiencing declining living standards.[39]

Mounting pressures on the European project—a global recession, a migrant crisis, and terrorist attacks—have highlighted an alarming divide between the ambitions of the European Union's economic and political arrangements and their public support. In the wake of mounting challenges to the Union, populists have gained traction by vowing to protect their constituencies from growing economic and cultural insecurities through a reinvigorated nationalism.

Benedict Anderson famously wrote that nationalism rests on the idea of the nation as an "imagined community." The community is "imagined" because in order to identify with it, we must convince ourselves that in sharing a nation, we inherently possess a unique sense of belonging with other members of the nation even though most of them remain complete strangers to us. In an effort to achieve regional integration, the European Union has attempted to foster an "imagined community" at the supranational level. But nationalism remains the prevailing form of collective imagination.

As the political theorist Alan Finlayson writes, "While part of the logic of community is to swallow up and obliterate differences, communities are also always particular."[40] This fact is certainly not lost on today's populist challengers to the European transnational project.

In the 2014 speech in which he outlined his illiberal vision, Orban declared: "The Hungarian nation is not a simple sum of individuals, but a community that needs to be organized, strengthened, and developed."[41] In Orban's view, the chaotic and random "sum of individuals" represents European supranationalism, as distinct from populism's clarifying sense of national identity. The populist articulation of "the people" as belonging primarily to the nation has weakened efforts driven by the elite to popularize its concept of a European "people." The underdevelopment of European citizenship has allowed populists to depict Europe itself as a primary threat to the national communities that are solidly entrenched in the public imagination. By offering itself as the guardian of the nation, populism has emerged as an alternative to liberal democratic internationalism.

Not only populists make the case for the primacy of national loyalties. The French political theorist Pierre Manent has recently argued against what he characterizes as the "new orthodoxy" that only the individual and all of humanity have real moral weight, with nothing of worth in between. All of modern history suggests that the rise of democracy is indissolubly linked to the emergence of the nation-state. Although Benjamin Constant famously distinguished between the liberty of the moderns (freedom in the private sphere) and the liberty of the ancients (participation in communal self-determination), in practice they go together. As Manent puts it, "Only the representative government of a people formed into a nation" can make legitimate decisions about laws and rules. The traditional national framework of democracy in Europe does not guarantee any particular result; the people will not always be virtuous and far-sighted. But Manent insists that "nothing humanly decent is possible outside this framework."[42]

This is not to say that the boundaries of political identification are fixed. The formation of France testifies to the contrary, as does the creation of the United States from colonies with distinctive independent histories. But as both of these cases suggest, expanding formal political boundaries is no guarantee that public sentiments will follow. Overcoming French regional loyalties required centuries; in the United States, subordinating state loyalties to a shared national loyalty took not only time but also a bloody civil war.

Transnationalism is not the cure for populism. It is better understood as a cause of populism. The antidote to populism must include a decent, responsible nationalism, shorn of populism's nativism and its anti-pluralist fantasies of a homogeneous people.

FIVE

Is Democracy at Risk in the United States?

I will never forget June 23, 2016, the date of the Brexit vote. I stayed up most of the night watching the BBC, absorbing the mounting shock of political commentators and elected officials as the returns trickled in. Not even Nigel Farage, the father of the United Kingdom Independence Party, who had campaigned for decades against Britain's membership in the European Union, could believe the results. Early in the evening he had issued a statement of concession, which he happily retracted some hours later.

In the wee hours of the morning, a thought flashed through my mind: with different accents and a change of proper nouns, the worthies of the BBC could have been talking about the American presidential campaign. The issues were similar, as were the grievances and demographic divides. Donald Trump began calling himself "Mr. Brexit." I took him seriously; I should have taken him literally as well.

Postelection studies of the British vote have clarified its principal dynamics. A synthesis of the research shows that "education levels appear to have been the single biggest driver of the decision to either Leave or Remain."[1] While 73 percent of voters with college and advanced degrees voted to remain, 75 percent of voters who left the British equivalent of high school without passing standard exit exams voted to leave.[2] Not only does higher education expand one's opportunities, it also shapes one's outlook.

All else being equal, individuals with higher education tend to favor openness, variety, and innovation. They are more open to demographic change and internationalism, and they tend to value creativity and curiosity over order and discipline. Highly educated individuals are more likely to believe that they have options in life and that they retain a measure of control over their own fate. Less educated people are more likely to see themselves as lacking control over their own lives, a sentiment that political psychologists have linked to the desire for order and authority.

Other key drivers of the Brexit vote included income, age, place, immigration, and economic sector. Older, lower-income voters from smaller cities and rural areas were more likely to favor leaving the European Union, as were those from manufacturing regions and areas that had seen a rapid surge in immigration during the past decade. A majority of citizens who considered themselves middle class voted to remain in the Union, while a majority of self-identified working-class citizens voted to leave it.[3]

It is a mistake, researchers agreed, to overemphasize the role of economics in the outcome. Rather, voters viewed the events of the past two decades through a multifaceted prism of culture, values, and sentiments. As the political scientists Matthew Goodwin and Oliver Heath put it, the Brexit vote was "anchored predominantly, albeit not exclusively, in areas of the country that are filled with pensioners, low-skilled and less well-educated blue-collar workers and citizens who have been pushed to the margins not only by the economic transformation of the country, but by the values that have come to dominate a more socially liberal media and political class."[4]

Immigration too was more than an economic issue: for many voters, the previous decade's rapid pace of immigration—especially from Eastern and Central Europe—posed unwelcome challenges to both cultural stability and national sovereignty.[5] If economics had been dominant, as the leaders of the Remain campaign assumed, the United Kingdom might not have opted to leave the European Union. When the Leave campaign focused more sharply on immigration and sovereignty, the tide turned in its direction.

Geography also mattered in surprising ways. It turns out that the size and diversity of social networks had a significant impact on attitude toward Brexit. Individuals who had socialized with people from another country, another part of Britain, or even another town were more likely to favor remaining in the European Union, while those whose social relations were confined to their own communities were more likely to vote Leave.[6]

Leave and Remain voters differed greatly in their attitudes toward the past and future of the United Kingdom. Leave voters believed that their children's generation would do worse than they themselves had done, while Remain voters were more optimistic. Fifty-eight percent of Leave supporters felt that life in Britain was worse than it was thirty years before, while 73 percent of Remain supporters thought it was better.[7]

Brexit voters reported a marked sense of political disenfranchisement. Many felt politicians had neglected their local areas and that the national government did not listen to their concerns. Brexit was popular among those who did not typically vote; many Leave voters had long withdrawn trust from government and elected officials and had not participated in the 2015 general election.[8] In this atmosphere of mistrust, these voters were drawn to conspiracy theories about collaboration between British intelligence services, the government, and the European Union to prevent a Brexit vote. This mistrust extended to the vote itself. One survey found that half of Leave voters believed the election might be rigged, versus 11 percent of Remain supporters.[9]

There was, finally, an international dimension to the public attitudes shaping the outcome. Those who favored cooperation with other countries were 52 percentage points more likely to favor remaining in Europe than were those who thought Britain is better off when it puts its own interests first "without worrying what other countries think." Not surprisingly, those who opposed compromise were also more likely to favor leaders they regarded as strong and principled rather than consensual and conciliatory.[10]

The Populist Surge in the United States

I need not dwell, I suspect, on the multiple resonances between the Brexit vote and Donald Trump's remarkable rise to the presidency of the United States. A detailed analysis of U.S. exit polls as well as postelection survey research reinforces most people's qualitative first impressions. Still, each country is different. The response of Americans to their country's economic, social, and political dysfunction has set the stage for a distinctively American populism.

Economy

The poor performance of the economy, at least as average Americans have experienced it, has framed the politics of the past generation. After seven consecutive years of growth following the recession of the early 1990s, median household income peaked in 1999.[11] Since then there has been no growth whatsoever. In mid-2017, eight years after the official end of the Great Recession, median household income barely exceeded the 2007 Bush-era peak and roughly equaled the level of the late 1990s.

After the previous peak in 1989, household income declined for four years, bottoming out in 1993. By 1996 it had regained all the lost ground, and it continued to surge for years afterward. In the sixteen years from 1983 to 1999, median household income rose by nearly nine thousand dollars—more than 18 percent.[12] There is no postwar parallel for the stagnation Americans have experienced during the past generation.

Making matters worse, the economic pain has been unevenly divided. By virtually every measure, metropolitan areas have done much better than small towns and rural areas. For example, aggregate employment in metropolitan America is 5 percent above its peak prior to the Great Recession, while nonmetropolitan employment remains substantially lower than at the end of 2007, right before the bottom fell out.[13] The sharp decline in U.S. manufacturing employment since the beginning of the century has been concentrated in the country's heartland, while the postindustrial coastal economies have suffered much less damage.

A glance at recent economic history underscores the magnitude of this shift. During the first five years of recovery from the recession of 1990–91, rural and small-town counties were responsible for 63 percent of newly generated jobs. In the five years after the 2001 recession, the results were comparable, with 59 percent of new jobs located in these less populated counties. But in the first five years after the Great Recession, only 35 percent of job gains were in these counties, versus 64 percent in counties with populations of five hundred thousand or more. During these two decades, the share of new jobs in counties dominated by large cities more than doubled, from only 16 percent in the early and middle 1990s to 41 percent between 2010 and 2014. This massive shift of jobs, income, and wealth to urban centers has not gone unnoticed, and it has fed rural and small-town Americans' sense of being left out and ignored.[14]

To a greater extent than in other Western democracies, trade enters into the American narrative of economic decline. Americans blame the North American Free Trade Agreement for the development of continental supply chains that shifted manufacturing production to Mexico. The entry of China into the World Trade Organization accelerated the growth of its exports to the United States, and the regions most exposed to Chinese import penetration experienced the largest losses of manufacturing jobs and wages.[15] In this context, Donald Trump's denunciation of the entire postwar trade regime found a receptive audience.

The past generation's economic performance has underlined longer-term changes in opportunity and mobility in the United States. Children born into middle-income households in 1940 had a better than nine-in-ten chance of outperforming their parents by the time they reached the age of thirty. But fewer than half the children born in the 1980s were doing better than their parents thirty years later.[16] Little changes if incomes are compared at the age of forty rather than thirty.

This multigenerational economic change has profoundly affected public attitudes. The heart of the "American Dream" is progress—the expectation by parents that their children will do better than they have. But a 2015 Pew Research Center survey found that only 32 percent of Americans expressed such optimism about the next generation, compared to 60 percent who thought the next generation would be worse off.[17]

The public outlook was bleaker in nearly every country in Europe. Only 15 percent of Italians and 14 percent of French respondents thought the next generation would enjoy a better future.[18] But optimism has never been as central to European societies as it has been in the United States, whose citizens have experienced a profound shock to long-held expectations.

Society

Ever since the countercultural eruption that began in the late 1960s, American society has been divided about issues such as abortion, illegal drugs, the role of religion in politics, and—most recently— the proper legal status for sexual orientations and acts outside the boundaries of heterosexuality. Frequently these divisions have figured centrally in national political contests, but while they have by no means disappeared, their impact on political debate in the past two years has diminished, overlaid by rising concerns about the impact of immigration on the U.S. population.

These concerns fall into three categories. Many Americans with lower levels of education and skills believe that poorly educated immigrants, especially from Mexico and Central America, are competing for increasingly scarce low-skilled jobs and are driving down working-class wages. Higher-than-average unemployment rates among lower-skilled workers and a decades-long reduction in their incomes have reinforced this belief.

Next come demographic concerns, which a brief history can frame. The surge of immigration around the turn of the twentieth century raised the share of first-generation immigrants to 15 percent of the population, triggering a nativist reaction that culminated in the restrictive immigration legislation of 1924. Over the next four decades, the first-generation share declined by two- thirds, bottoming out at 4.7 percent in the early 1960s. The political salience of ethnic differences within the white majority faded.[19]

In 1965, the landmark Hart-Celler Bill reopened the gates and allowed large numbers of immigrants from long-excluded areas such as East Asia and the Indian subcontinent, as well as from the Spanish-speaking countries of the Americas. The consequence over the past five decades has been a demographic revolution. Millions of nonwhite, non-European immigrants have entered U.S. society. Latinos and Asians are the fastest-growing groups, while the white share of the population is shrinking steadily. Three states (including California and Texas, the two largest) already have majority-minority populations, and many more will join them in the coming decades. By 2044, if current trends continue, the United States as a whole will no longer have a white majority, as "white" is now defined.[20]

To be sure, previous generations of immigrants from Central and southern Europe—Poles, Hungarians, Czechs, and Italians, among others—gradually blended into, and identified with, the overall population. But this process occurred during an extended period when new immigration had slowed to a trickle and first-generation immigrants represented a steadily declining share of the population —the reverse of the situation that now prevails.

This ongoing demographic shift has triggered palpable anxiety among many native-born Americans, especially those outside the metropolitan areas that have always served as immigration gateways. These Americans have a sense, understandable in light of their experience, that they are the rightful owners of the country and that new entrants threaten their control. Although they express their anxiety most often as anger against the roughly eleven million immigrants who are present in the United States illegally, many also believe that current levels of legal immigration are too high and should be reduced.

Finally, security concerns weigh heavily on many voters' minds. During the 2016 presidential campaign, Donald Trump asserted that immigrants from Mexico increase the U.S. crime rate and that immigrants from Muslim-majority countries constitute a terrorist threat. Although policies such as mass deportation and a ban on Muslim immigration never received majority support, a substantial minority of Americans regarded them as justified.

The threat of crime and terrorism creates a pervasive sense of insecurity. In surveys taken in June 2016, 86 percent of Americans expressed concern about so-called lone wolf terrorist attacks, and only 31 percent had confidence in the government's ability to prevent them. It is easy to understand why the desired balance between security and civil liberty is shifting. The same surveys revealed 54 percent of Americans worried that the government would not do enough to monitor the activities of "potential terrorists," compared to 39 percent who feared that the government would go too far. Seventy-two percent favored increased surveillance of people suspected of possible links to terrorism, even if it would intrude on privacy rights.[21]

Politics

The dysfunction of the American political system is well enough known to require only brief remarks. Suffice it to say that over the past quarter century the two major political parties have become more polarized—that is, both more internally homogeneous and more ideologically distant from each other. As this process has proceeded, the adherents of the respective parties have tended to cluster geographically, a phenomenon the sociologist Bill Bishop has dubbed the "Big Sort."[22] Combined with the decline of transpartisan broadcasting and the rise of politically inflected media, this sorting has produced the social equivalent of echo chambers in which partisans are increasingly likely to hear only the opinions with which they agree and to encounter only the evidence consistent with these opinions.

Polarization is affective as well as cognitive. For the first time in the history of modern survey research, majorities of partisans have not merely an unfavorable but a deeply unfavorable view of the other party. In a 2016 survey, 49 percent of Republicans reported that the Democratic Party makes them afraid, and 46 percent that it made them angry. The sentiments of Democrats were even more intense: 55 percent said the Republican Party made them afraid, and 47 percent that it made them angry. Forty-seven percent of Republicans see Democrats as more "immoral" than other Americans; 70 percent of Democrats see Republicans as more "closed-minded." Forty-five percent of Republicans view Democratic policies as not only misguided but also a "threat," up from 37 percent in 2014, while 41 percent of Democrats see Republican policies as threatening, up from 31 percent in 2014. Among both sides' most engaged and active partisans, these figures are even higher.[23]

In a remarkable inversion of the feminist dictum that the personal is political, it now seems that the political has become personal. Large numbers of Americans are troubled that their child might marry someone of the opposite political persuasion. A fiftieth-anniversary remake of Stanley Kramer's *Guess Who's Coming to Dinner* would feature a Trump-supporting boyfriend at the table of an upscale liberal family, or vice versa.

In a parliamentary system, these polarities, though troubling, would at least be manageable. In the U.S. constitutional system, which allows for divided control of different national institutions, they are much more problematic. Partisan polarization makes compromise difficult, and so the typical consequence of divided government is gridlock. In contemporary circumstances, the national government can act effectively only when all its powers are in the hands of a single party. But then the dominant party is likely to go it alone and implement its preferred program, whatever the minority thinks. Few single-party governments resist the temptation to overreach. Winston Churchill's injunction—in victory, magnanimity—is ignored. So the cycle of gridlock yielding public dissatisfaction producing unified government giving way to partisan overreach followed by public reaction producing divided government and renewed gridlock continues indefinitely.

Although unified government can produce unbalanced and unsustainable public policy, gridlock is a greater threat to the democratic order. In their efforts to govern effectively, presidents are tempted to extend their powers beyond constitutional bounds. Worse, an impatient populace becomes more willing to set aside the restraints inherent in the rule of law. In a June 2016 survey conducted by the Public Religion Research Institute, 49 percent of voters agreed with the statement "Because things have gotten so far off track in this country, we need a leader who is willing to break some rules if that's what it takes to set things right." This figure included 57 percent of Republicans, 60 percent of white working-class voters, 72 percent of Trump supporters, and—tellingly—59 percent of those who felt that the American way of life needs protection from foreign influences.[24]

The Populist Response to Dysfunction

Many ordinary citizens hold American elites (often of both political parties) responsible for what has gone wrong over the past generation, and there is some basis for their view. While experts enjoyed a rare period of deference between the end of World War II and the mid-1960s, policy failures since then, both at home and abroad, have weakened their claims. The "best and the brightest" led the United States into Vietnam. The intelligence community's consensus that Saddam Hussein possessed weapons of mass destruction smoothed the path to war in Iraq. Financial experts engineered new forms of investment that helped bring on the Great Recession.

At the same time that trust in expertise has declined, meritocratic norms and practices have propelled highly educated Americans to the highest reaches of the economy, media, and politics. This group has benefited from the transition to a knowledge-based economy as well as from freer flows of goods, people, and capital. On the other hand, leaders have made at best half-hearted efforts to insulate average Americans from the negative consequences of these trends or to compensate them for their losses. Worse, many leaders have appeared oblivious to the travails of their fellow citizens, and this blindness is often tinged with meritocratic snobbery toward those with less education and status.

The phrase "flyover country" perfectly captures the outlook of bicoastal elites, and the citizens of flyover country took their revenge in 2016. Who were these voters, and why did Trump's message resonate?

Rather than securing victory through the uncompromising support of a homogeneous voting bloc, Trump won the general election by assembling a coalition of voters with diverse political ideologies and personal circumstances. Yet one group stands out for its early and sustained enthusiasm. These core supporters of Trump made up a fifth of his general election voters and were responsible for his initial unexpected rise (82 percent of them voted for him in the GOP primaries). Members of this group are economically progressive and overwhelmingly support increasing the tax rate for the wealthy, believe the system is rigged against people like them, and hold strong anti-immigrant and ethnocentric views.[25]

They are the least educated and earn the lowest incomes among Trump's general election voters. They are the most likely to receive Medicaid benefits, to report a disability that interferes with employment opportunities, to spend many hours watching TV every day, and to be categorized as politically uninformed. Perhaps surprising to some, they are not staunch social conservatives. Only 33 percent describe themselves as pro-life, and few are gun owners or NRA members. They are not even passionate partisans. Fifty-three percent want to see their member of Congress legislate on a bipartisan basis to get things done. Of the members of the Trump coalition, these voters were the most likely to have voted for Barack Obama in 2012.[26]

While his populism upended some established right-left political divisions, Trump also benefited from a shift in the party coalitions that began before his candidacy. Between 2012 and 2016, this group of core Trump supporters shifted thirteen points toward the Republican Party. While white voters without a college education had split their votes almost evenly during the 1990s between the Democratic and Republican parties, by 2015, 57 percent of these voters identified as Republican and only 33 percent as Democrat. This "diploma divide" marks one of the most significant changes in today's party landscape.[27]

An examination of white vote switchers (those who voted for Obama in 2012 and for Trump in 2016) finds that attitudes on immigration and racial and religious minorities dominated voters' decision-making. For example, 33 percent of white Obama voters characterized illegal immigrants as a "drain," and 34 percent favored making it harder for foreigners to come to the United States. Staunch opposition to a pathway to citizenship for illegal immigrants motivated many to switch to Trump in 2016. Similarly, the 37 percent of white Obama voters holding less favorable attitudes toward Muslims and reporting negative perceptions of African Americans were also likely to favor Trump in 2016. Compared to 2012, 2016 saw a much tighter relationship between the attitudes of voters on identity issues and their choice of candidate.[28]

Throughout the 2016 campaign, a debate persisted over whether economic anxiety or cultural backlash explained support for Trump. Some argued that populist disaffection fundamentally stems from economic insecurity and therefore marks an effort to ameliorate woes caused by deindustrialization and globalization. Others argued the election demonstrated a powerful resurgence of overtly racist and xenophobic attitudes.

Postelection survey research demonstrates that voters' economic anxiety does not offer an adequate explanation of the 2016 election.[29] But there does appear to be some relation between financial insecurity and anti-immigrant or ethnocentric views. One comprehensive study shows that white survey respondents who thought the economy was getting worse in 2012 were more likely in 2016 to believe it should be more difficult for foreigners to immigrate, to characterize immigration as a drain on the country, and to hold negative views toward Muslims, regardless of their responses to the same survey questions in 2012. This general relationship persisted when considering perceptions voters had of their personal financial situation in 2012: voters who reported they were struggling financially were more likely in 2016 to hold negative views of immigrants and Muslims, regardless of their responses in 2012.[30]

While today's populism poses a challenge to the classic Marxist framework in which economic structures and relations determine a society's political and cultural life, it would be wrong, in analyzing the causes of Trump's rise, to dismiss the views that voters had of the economy and the economic well-being of their families and communities. There is a complex interaction among economic, cultural, and security factors, each of which independently affects public attitudes.

As I argue at length in this book's concluding chapter, an element of tribal thinking is inherent in the human condition. When economic times are good and citizens feel personally secure, tribal sentiments remain muted: there are no urgent problems for which the Other need be blamed. But either a sharp downturn or a pressing security threat can activate these sentiments. When both occur simultaneously, tribalism surges. When demographic change is added to the mix, We/They thinking can dominate public consciousness. And as we have seen, this sharp dichotomy is the breeding ground of populism.

Is American Democracy in Danger?

The public sentiments behind the populist explosion have been building for many years. Since the 1970s—with a few temporary interruptions during the economic boom of the late 1990s and again in the wake of the 9/11 attacks—public trust and confidence in national governmental institutions has hovered between 20 and 30 percent.[31] The most recent survey found that only 20 percent of Americans, close to the historic low, trust the federal government to do what's right all or most of the time.[32] Half a century ago, this figure stood near 75 percent.

At the same time, Americans' views concerning the motives of elected officials have darkened. Half a century ago, nearly two-thirds of Americans believed the federal government was run for the benefit of all the people. By the end of 2015, only 19 percent of Americans held this view.[33]

More recently, other major institutions such as banks, large corporations, and the news media have lost the public's trust. Today, surveys find that the public regards only a handful of institutions— the U.S. military, colleges and universities, churches and religious organizations, technology companies, and small businesses—as making a positive contribution to the country.

For decades, researchers have monitored Americans' overall assessment of their country's trajectory. One survey asks respondents to assess whether the nation is generally headed in the right direction or if things have gone off on the wrong track; another version asks whether respondents are satisfied or dissatisfied with the way things are going in the United States. Despite differences of methodology, the results are remarkably consistent. In the final five years of the twentieth century, solid majorities of Americans were positive about the direction of the country. But since 2004, despite multiple changes in party control of Congress and the White House, majorities have been consistently negative.[34]

As this book goes to press, the election of Donald Trump has not disrupted these trends. Much will depend on his ability to make good on his promises to the white working-class voters whose overwhelming support largely gave him his victory. Repealing Obamacare, whose Medicaid expansion disproportionately bene-fited working-class voters in Republican-dominated states, would not have reopened shuttered coal mines and steel mills. A classic Republican tax cut will not revitalize declining Rust Belt communi-ties. It remains to be seen whether the small-government Republi-cans who dominate Congress will be willing to fund the president's $1 trillion infrastructure buildup, the most broadly popular policy component of his populist appeal.

There are signs of impatience with liberal democratic restraints in the United States, where constitutionalism and the rule of law are more deeply entrenched than in the newer European democra-cies. In two pathbreaking articles, Roberto Foa and Yascha Mounk have presented survey research suggesting declining support in America for liberal democracy and a rising willingness to consider alternatives.[35]

Still, the connection between public attitudes and policy out-comes is loose. In times of intense concern about national or per-sonal security, Americans have often expressed doubts about the scope of individual liberty. In the aftermath of 9/11, for example, a 49 percent plurality agreed that the freedoms guaranteed by the First Amendment went "too far." These reservations were never translated into permanent reductions in personal liberty, and by 2006 the share of Americans who believed First Amendment liber-ties were too expansive had fallen to 18 percent.[36] American institu-tions have served as bulwarks against inconstant public attitudes, and when institutions fail—as the Supreme Court did when it upheld the internment of Japanese Americans during World War II—second thoughts by elites and eventually the public have usually reversed the damage.

If modern survey research had been available during the 1930s, it would probably have shown support for liberal democracy at a low ebb and substantial levels of sympathy for both communism and fascism. In his First Inaugural Address, President Franklin Roosevelt made it clear that the national economic emergency might require a "temporary departure from [the] normal balance of . . . executive and legislative authority." If halfway measures proved insufficient, he said, he would not hesitate to ask Congress for "broad executive power" to wage war against the emergency "as if we were in fact invaded by a foreign foe."[37] He did not say what he would do if Congress refused to go along. Fortunately, new policies and institutions within the constitutional framework proved equal to the task of preserving liberal democracy. No doubt FDR's assessment of the American people's underlying devotion to the constitutional order, whatever their temporary doubts, strengthened his own commitment.

The question is whether U.S. institutions and norms will prove strong enough to outlast, and if necessary resist, today's challenge to liberal democracy.

A moment of testing comes when the judiciary hands down a ruling that prevents the president from doing what he wants or orders him to do something he does not want. When the Supreme Court told President Truman that he could not seize the steel mills, he backed down. When it told President Nixon to hand over the Oval Office tapes, he complied. Notably, when the federal courts told President Trump that his executive order on immigrants and refugees did not meet constitutional standards, he accepted their verdict and drafted a revised order that he hoped would fare better.

Tensions between the executive and judicial branches often escalate when steps taken to enhance national security restrict individual liberty. In the aftermath of the 9/11 attacks, George W. Bush's administration dealt with detained terrorist suspects in ways that the Supreme Court ruled violated constitutional rights. The administration accepted these judgments. Democracy in the United

States would enter new and dangerous territory if a president did not.

Another moment of testing for liberal democracy would come if an administration infringed on freedom of the press. Since the Supreme Court permitted the publication of the Pentagon Papers, it has been taken for granted that the executive branch cannot invoke claims of national security to prevent the media from making classified information public. Still, an administration could threaten other means—such as tax audits and regulatory crackdowns—to pursue the same end. Relations between presidents and the press almost always turn adversarial, and an all-out assault on the press led by the president could do lasting damage to American democracy. While the attack by President Trump on the media as "enemies of the people" was hardly helpful, his words are not enough to create a crisis for democracy.

Most Americans have a hard time believing that their democracy is at risk of what Foa and Mounk call deconsolidation, and they have centuries of history on their side. The constitutional order has survived the no-holds-barred battle between the Federalists and the Jeffersonians, the Civil War, the Great Depression of the 1930s, the assassinations and cultural upheavals of the 1960s, and the security panic that swept the country after the 9/11 attacks. During the two world wars of the twentieth century, both of which evoked national mobilizations, liberal restraints on government were weakened only temporarily. Freedom of the press survived the Alien and Sedition Acts of the 1790s, the Espionage and Sedition Acts of 1917–18, and the clashes of the Nixon era. The ethos of individual liberty has always been a powerful countervailing force. Besides, the greatest challenges to constitutional democracy have always come during wars or national emergencies, and current circumstances, however distressing, do not rise to this level.

Developments since President Trump's election suggest that America's constitutional institutions once again are proving equal to the task. The judiciary has acted with characteristic independence. The press is doing its job in the face of unrelenting pressure from the administration and its supporters. The long-supine Congress is showing signs of standing up and strengthening its backbone. Ideological and geographical differences within the Republican Party have impeded its efforts to put unified government in the service of a conservative agenda that lacks majority support. Madison's nightmare of a tyrannical concentration of power seems as distant as ever.

Nevertheless, events at home and abroad have been a salutary warning against progressivist complacency. History does not have an end; nor does it arc toward justice. Liberal democracy is not self-sustaining. It is a human achievement, not a historical inevitability. Like every human creation, it can be weakened from within when those who support it do not rally to its cause.

That an event has never happened is no guarantee that it will not happen. Eternal vigilance is indeed the price of liberty, and liberal democracy will endure as long as citizens believe it is worth fighting for. Despite some troubling signs, most Americans still think it is, and support for the key institutions that protect the country from tyranny remains strong. Newer democracies, where liberal norms are less firmly entrenched, could be a different story.[38]

As this book went to press, the ANO Party, founded and led by billionaire businessman Andrej Babiš, won the Czech election with almost 30 percent of the vote. Babiš campaigned against immigration, Brussels, and government corruption. He favors constitutional changes that would reduce checks on executive power, and he has stated, "The [ANO] party is connected to my person. The party is me." There is a distinct possibility that he could end up leading his country's hard-won democracy down the illiberal trail that Hungary and Poland have blazed.

SIX

Liberal Democracy in America

What Is to Be Done?

Vigorous economic growth is necessary for broadly shared prosperity, but it is not sufficient. We thought otherwise during the three decades after World War II because we overlooked the special circumstances that translated growth into an expanding middle class. The war had destroyed the economies of Europe and Japan, leaving the United States in a position without parallel in modern history. Domestic production accounted for nearly all the goods and services Americans consumed, and consumption accounted for nearly all the revenues flowing into corporate coffers. In this quasi-closed economy, labor, capital, and government could combine to shape wages and prices. President John F. Kennedy could compel steel companies to retract what the government regarded as destabilizing price increases, and powerful unions could bargain industry-wide to boost wages and benefits. U.S. consumers had little choice but to accept the prices that flowed from this quasi-corporatist process, but rising real wages made rising prices palatable, and rapid productivity gains helped ward off a wage-price spiral.

The slow collapse of this postwar economic arrangement is an oft-told tale. Suffice it to say that as the economies of America's Second World War allies and adversaries recovered, U.S. firms encountered increasing foreign competition, first from basic consumer goods that could be produced more cheaply abroad using low-cost labor, then from products higher up the value chain. This challenge changed the game for U.S. producers, who faced new incentives to restrain costs. They responded by locating production facilities in lower-wage jurisdictions, at home and then abroad, and also by replacing human labor with productivity-boosting technology. These moves reduced the size and influence of the private-sector unions. The collapse of the USSR and the emergence of China and India integrated two billion new workers into the global economy, further ratcheting up the pressure on jobs and wages.

As U.S. firms became increasingly global, they derived a higher share of their revenues from consumers outside the United States, and they came to care less about their relations with the U.S. cities and communities in which their headquarters were located. When Charles Wilson, CEO of General Motors and President Eisenhower's nominee for secretary of defense, appeared before the Senate Armed Services Committee in 1953 for his confirmation hearing, he explained his past conduct with an often-misquoted sentence: "For years I thought what was good for the country was good for General Motors, and vice versa."[1] There is no reason to doubt his sincerity, and much evidence in favor of the linkage he discerned.

Half a century later, the relationship between corporate interests and the national interest is more tenuous. The interplay of globalization and technological change fundamentally shifted the balance between labor and capital, setting in motion the slow erosion of the postwar middle class. As labor economists have shown, what had been an occupational bell curve shifted toward a bifurcated pattern, with high-skilled workers at one end and low-paid workers in retail, food, and personal services at the other. Jobs requiring mid-level skills and offering mid-level compensation became relatively scarce. The Great Recession and its aftermath accelerated this hollowing out of the U.S. workforce.

Meanwhile, the now-famous 1 percent was breaking away from the pack. The gap between the compensation of corporate leaders and the wages of their workers increased many times over, and the surge of the financial sector produced a new tranche of packagers, traders, and managers who enjoy almost unimaginable wealth.

These trends have sparked debate over rising inequality. Some serious economists assert a link between higher inequality and slower growth; others discount it. Some philosophers affirm that these levels of inequality are morally wrong; others deny it. What is not in doubt is that conditions for less educated workers and their families have worsened, while middle-class families have been treading water at best. Many parents fear that their children will do worse than they did, in part because they find it difficult to finance postsecondary education.

Although trained and educated workers do better than those who are less prepared, education and training no longer guarantee a rising standard of living. (Allowing for inflation, median annual earnings of workers with B.A.s have not increased in recent decades.)[2] During the postwar boom, nearly all workers could expect to do better than their parents. In recent decades, barely half have done so, and belief in the American Dream has waned.

In these circumstances, and given current policies, there is no reason to expect that conditions will improve for the middle class, let alone those lower down on the ladder. U.S. public policy has no choice but to lean harder against the economic wind, both to accelerate economic growth and to ensure that its fruits are widely shared. At long last, our leaders must turn away from peripheral squabbles and attend to the one issue that more than any other will define our country's future.

Accelerating Growth

In retrospect, it is clear that the dawn of the twenty-first century represented an inflection point for the U.S. economy. Between 1949 and 2000, Third Way's Jim Kessler calculates, the annual rate of growth exceeded 3 percent thirty-four times—two years out of every three. During the eight Clinton years, growth reached 4 percent five times and fell below 3 percent only twice. Since 2000, growth has reached 3 percent just twice and has never reached 4 percent, even during 2003–7, the peak years of the Bush recovery from the 2001 recession. Since the beginning of the recovery from the Great Recession, annual growth has not reached 3 percent even once. Between 1949 and 2000, the economy grew at an average rate of 3.6 percent annually. Since then, growth has averaged 1.8 percent—only half as fast.[3]

In our present economic circumstances, only a sustained period of robust growth will be enough to raise wages and household incomes. Unless the economy can grow faster than it has since the end of the twentieth century, U.S. workers will be hard pressed to regain the ground they have lost, let alone offer the prospects of something better for their children. Even if we are unsure exactly how to accelerate growth, we have an obligation to try harder. This will mean, among other measures, expanding the share of Americans in the paid workforce; boosting the public and private investments essential for more rapid productivity gains; and revising legal and regulatory restraints whose economic costs clearly outweigh their social benefits.

Sharing the Fruits of Growth

As recent decades have demonstrated, no mechanism automatically translates economic growth into broadly shared prosperity. If we increase the pace of growth without widening its beneficiaries, we will do little to strengthen the middle class and enhance social mobility. Accomplishing this second task requires pursuing three key objectives: adopting full employment as a principal goal of economic policy; restoring the link between productivity gains and wage increases; and treating earned and unearned income equally in our tax code.

Full Employment

The second half of the 1990s was the last time that economic groups from top to bottom progressed together at roughly the same rate. It is no coincidence that during this period the labor market reached and then sustained full employment, improving workers' bargaining power and bringing previously neglected individuals back into the workforce. This history suggests that we should adopt full employment as a high-priority goal of economic policy and should welcome the wage increases it would generate. Because global competition makes it difficult for businesses to raise prices, wage increases would likely come out of profits, which now stand at a record share of national income. This might prove problematic if businesses lacked capital for investment, but they don't. Large firms in particular are accumulating huge stocks of retained earnings that languish on the sidelines or are used to fund mergers and stock buybacks.

Full employment means more than minimizing the official unemployment rate; it means also maximizing Americans' participation in the labor force. Since 2000, and especially since 2007, labor force participation has fallen farther than can be explained by an aging population. Women's participation peaked in the late 1990s and has been declining ever since. Men aged twenty-five to fifty-four—their prime working years—are less likely to be in the paid workforce than they were a generation ago.

Full employment is more than an economic good; it is a moral imperative. In modern societies, work not only provides a livelihood; it also gives our lives structure and purpose, and it is a key source of self-confidence and social respect. It promotes stable families and healthy communities and strengthens the bonds of trust between individuals and their governing institutions. Conversely, we know all too well the consequences of long-term unemployment: diminished self-respect, increased strife within families, epidemics of substance abuse, blighted neighborhoods, and a corrosive sense of helplessness.

When hyperinflation or financial collapse dominates the economic landscape, it may be necessary temporarily to subordinate full employment to the short-term imperatives of the crisis and its stabilization. Absent such extreme circumstances, however, full employment should stand at the center of long-term economic policies.

Relinking Productivity and Wages

We should do what we can to restore the relationship between wage increases and productivity gains. Laws and regulations should encourage profit sharing and worker ownership. Firms that share the benefits of productivity increases with their workers should enjoy tax and other advantages relative to firms whose executives and shareholders pocket the gains while ignoring their workforce.

The balance between wages and profits affects growth as well as distribution. In the long run, workers cannot spend more than they are paid. As wage growth slowed in recent decades, middle-class families kept up their living standards first by sending women into the workforce and then by taking on additional debt, in part drawn from the equity they had accumulated from rising home prices. When the housing bubble burst, these families suffered an economic shock that drove many into bankruptcy and induced most of the middle class to reduce debt and live on earned income. The recovery since the end of the Great Recession has been the weakest of the entire postwar period largely because household and family incomes have taken so long to recover. Only wage increases can generate more vigorous growth, and if market mechanisms fail to produce higher wages, public policy should step in.

Ending Preferential Tax Treatment for Unearned Income
There is no reason why the tax code should give additional advantages to the wealthy, whom the market is already treating extremely well. We should adopt a strong presumption against tax provisions that treat some sources of income more favorably than wages and salaries. Tax expenditures that disproportionately benefit upper-income investors should be scrapped or redirected toward the middle class. While providing incentives for new investment may serve the public interest, it is hard to understand why the winner of a bet about the future value of existing equity or debt should be treated better than an ordinary wage earner. Capital gains should be treated preferentially only when they come from transactions that increase the aggregate of productively invested capital—for example, when investors provide new capital for start-ups or rapidly expanding businesses.

Connecting Rural Regions to Metropolitan Centers
Throughout the market democracies of the West, remote and less densely populated regions are losing ground to metropolitan centers. Agricultural areas can still do well when commodity prices are high, but the light industries that once thrived in smaller communities have weakened in the face of competitive pressure. But more than that: it appears that the modern knowledge-based economy thrives on the density and diversity found in larger cities. Concentrations of educated professionals yield network effects that spur innovation.

Public policy cannot fully eliminate the rural/urban gap, which is rooted in basic features of the modern economy. But through expanded investment in infrastructure, governments can help small towns participate in the fruits of metropolitan growth. Improved transportation systems could enable people who work in cities to live farther from their workplaces without spending so many of their waking hours in lengthy commutes. If more educated professionals chose the tranquillity, safety, and lower housing prices that smaller towns can offer, their discretionary spending could boost local economies.

Information technology is another strategy for bridging the rural/urban gap. During the New Deal, the electrification of rural areas helped bring isolated communities into the national economy and society. Today that role is played by broadband connections. But many remote regions lack even a single internet provider. A national commitment to connect all homes, schools, businesses, and civil society organizations could expand opportunities in rural areas and small towns that feel abandoned and hopeless.

Economics and Future Generations in Market Democracies

New economic policies like these will accelerate economic growth and allow workers to share in its gains. But to treat the source of our current ills as purely economic is to understate the complexity of the challenge.

To recapitulate: the postwar liberal democratic bargain rested on the premise that elected governments could manage market economies to deliver broadly shared prosperity. The bargain that held for the first three decades after World War II waned over the next three as the standard formula for success—growth, private and public investment, innovation, an educated and trained workforce—lost much of its efficacy. During the 1920s and 1930s, the failure of market economies and democratic political institutions boosted the credibility of totalitarian governance and central planning. Today, after the Great Recession eroded the "Washington consensus," Chinese-style authoritarian state capitalism is becoming a more credible option for developing countries.

But—to pile complexity on complexity—it has taken more than globalization, technological change, and widening inequality to breach the postwar bargain. Another process has been at work as well: when market economies interact with democratic politics, public demands can slow growth in the name of other goods. For example, innovation is almost always disruptive, and people seek protection against the insecurity it creates. What begins as a safeguard against the downside of innovation can end up impeding innovation itself. Excessive credential requirements can prevent capable workers from entering the occupations of their choice. Rigid rules forcing employers to retain workers they no longer need may discourage them from hiring at all, forcing new entrants into the labor force to bear the brunt of change. This is one reason unemployment among young adults is so high in many European countries. Germany, which reformed its labor market early in the twenty-first century, stands out as an exception. Emmanuel Macron won the French presidency with a pledge to reform France's labor laws, among the most restrictive in Europe.

Resistance to innovation is hardly confined to incumbent workers. Existing companies, even whole industries, fiercely resist innovative competitors who threaten to disrupt established business models, and they do not hesitate to use their relationships with regulators and elected officials to strangle innovators in their cradles.

Social insurance is another source of security in market economies. During the past century, liberal democracies have created programs to provide income supplements during periods of unemployment, ensure an income stream during retirement, and protect against the economic consequences of illness. But in aging societies, the funding required for these programs can come at the expense of public investments needed for long-term economic growth—that is, unless governments are willing to raise taxes or tolerate higher budget deficits.

Even when public spending is robust, high levels of private consumption are needed to maintain economic vitality. Few individuals resist this, and why should they? Consumption yields convenience and pleasure. This generates another tension: the desire for a comfortable life is one of the forces suppressing birthrates in developed market economies. And when the population stagnates, growth slows.

In the mostly rural societies of the eighteenth and early nineteenth centuries, children were net economic assets. Even while still very young, they could work the land alongside their parents, contributing to household income. Today, children are expensive, and few adolescents can make significant economic contributions to their families, even when they are legally able to work. In the space of two centuries, childrearing has moved from a private good to a public good: although it yields emotional rewards, from a strictly economic standpoint it benefits society as a whole, while the parents bear most of the financial burden. Absent substantially increased public subsidies and assistance for those juggling the demands of parenthood and the paid workforce, fewer adults will choose to bear children, and those who do will bear fewer.

The challenge facing modern democracies is to establish a workable balance between past, present, and future. We must do our best to honor the promises we have made, whether to those who purchase public debt or those who rely on established programs for security in old age. We must provide enough buffers against economic shocks so that public discontent does not spill over into social disorder. But we must ensure that enough remains to make the investments and implement the innovations without which the future will be worse than the present. Doing this while strengthening the middle class and expanding opportunity for the working class will require the wealthy to bear more of the burden of funding social insurance programs.

Investing in the future is a tough sell in democratic politics. Leaders who promise short-term gains usually will enjoy an advantage over those who urge deferred consumption in the name of future improvement. But at the end of this road lies Venezuela's wrecked economy and bitterly divided society.

The preamble to the U.S. Constitution declares that a fundamental purpose of the Union is to secure the blessings of liberty for our posterity, not just ourselves. Edmund Burke famously defines society as a partnership "not only between those who are living, but between those who are living, those who are dead, and those who are to be born."[4] It is hard to believe that policies reflecting this premise will be accepted unless democratic publics feel some connection to posterity. "In the long run we are all dead" is an understandable epigram from a man who lived and died childless. But for society as a whole, it is a formula for slow-motion suicide.

Reconsidering the Link between Economic Growth and Liberal Democracy

Some environmentalists and traditional conservatives argue that all these difficulties can be traced back to the liberal democratic promise that popular governments can manage market economies so as to unleash unending material progress. Once that becomes the accepted metric of success, periods of economic distress are bound to weaken public support not just for markets but for liberal democracy itself as well.

There is some truth to this. But it is not a useful truth, because there is no possibility of turning back. I am hardly the first to observe that at the core of what we call modernity is the legitimation of the very human desire for a secure and comfortable existence. Because nature offers only the raw materials for such a life, realizing that desire requires ceaseless effort and ingenuity in the service of material improvement. As Aristotle observes in *Politics* (I.9), there is in principle no limit to such striving: "The desire for life being unlimited, [people] also desire in unlimited amount what is conducive to life."[5]

Only conceptions of good lives can limit boundless material striving, and only professions shaped by such conceptions can make the limits effective. Warriors who prize courage and loyalty are less concerned with material acquisition; so are scholars who seek truth and pious individuals who seek God.

But democracies have a hard time defining moral limits on acquisition. There is an inherent link between democracy and liberty, and between liberty and variety. In a democracy, Plato says in the *Republic* (VIII), one can speak freely and "do anything one pleases." The result is a wide variety of human characters and ways of life, "like a cloak embroidered with every kind of ornament."[6] Social norms are needed to secure peaceful coexistence in the face of these differences, but these are not the norms that would be needed to limit desire. Democracy is about expressing desire, not restraining it.

If so, then the liberal democratic bargain as I have defined it represents the modern means of fulfilling the inherent thrust of democracy itself. Abandoning the bargain will not bring about a more austere "steady-state" democracy. It will mean the end of modern democracy and its replacement by systems of government that are bound to be worse. In the end, leaders have no choice but to make the best of the bargain—to do what they can to restore public support for the means most conducive in the long run to the ends the people seek.

Immigration: Identity and Sovereignty

The link between inclusive economic growth and contemporary liberal democracy, though crucial, is only part of the story. Throughout the West in recent decades, public concerns about population flows across national borders have intensified. To some extent this trend reflects anxiety about economic displacement; the "Polish plumber" became a trope in the Brexit debate. Worries about the increased demand for social services have also played a part: Americans complain about tax burdens at the state and local levels, while British citizens fear that their cherished National Health Service is being overwhelmed.

But darker fears are also at work. The threat of Islamist terrorism directed at Western institutions and citizens has made these populations less willing to absorb new immigrants or even refugees from Muslim-majority countries. Citizens increasingly fear that Islam and liberal democracy are incompatible and that a clash of civilizations is inevitable. The issue of national identity is on the table, not only in scholarly debates, but also in the political arena. Those who believe that liberal democracy draws strength from diversity have been thrown on the defensive.

Large population flows, finally, have triggered concerns about the loss of national sovereignty. The European Union's unwillingness to compromise on the question of movement across its member nations' borders made it far more difficult for Britain's Remain forces to prevail against the public belief that control over immigration is a fundamental component of national sovereignty. In the United States, Donald Trump's famous promise to build a "big, beautiful wall" along the southern border became a powerful symbol of national sovereignty regained. A country that does not control its borders, he argued, is not fully a country, and enough Americans agreed with him to propel him into the White House.

But the concern extends beyond illegal immigration. After four decades of restrictive legislation, the 1965 reform act reopened the immigration gate and eliminated most national quotas. A half century later, the United States has been transformed demographically, and first-generation immigrants constitute 14 percent of the population, just shy of the peak a century ago. It should not be surprising that this latest cycle of immigration and the earlier one have evoked similar unease among American citizens, including many descendants of the previous wave's immigrants.

One may speculate that any country (even a self-styled nation of immigrants) has a finite capacity to absorb new arrivals, and that bumping up against this limit triggers a reaction that detractors condemn as nativist. In these circumstances, some adjustments are necessary and defensible. As Jeff Colgan and Robert Keohane put it, "It is not bigotry to calibrate immigration levels to the ability of immigrants to assimilate and to society's ability to adjust."[7]

In the United States, shifting away from family reunification and toward economic contribution as the main criterion for immigration would make sense politically as well as economically. So would an increased focus on the acquisition of English fluency and a working knowledge of American history and civic institutions. Acknowledging the legitimacy of widespread public concerns about the rule of law would ease the way for a reasonable and humane approach to the many millions of immigrants who are present illegally in the United States. One thing is clear: denouncing citizens concerned about immigration as ignorant and bigoted (as former British prime minister Gordon Brown did in an ill-fated election encounter with a potential supporter) does nothing to ameliorate either the substance of the problem or its politics.

Political Reform

Along with economics, identity, and sovereignty, political dysfunction is a trigger for populist discontent. The specifics of dysfunction vary among countries. Until recently in England and France, for example, it took the form of a center-left/center-right duopoly that limited the effective expression of views beyond its perimeter. In the United States, partisan antipathy has blocked policy responses to core public problems.

Despite such national differences, many Western democracies suffer from common political ills. The concentration of decision-making power in the center leads the periphery to feel distant and excluded. Concentrated wealth is viewed as influencing public decisions for its own benefit, and political insiders are seen as manipulating rules to serve themselves rather than the people. The consequence: corruption, a classic civic republican complaint.

Listing these ills is much easier than curing them. In Europe, the principal response to political duopoly is an outburst of activism on both the far left and the far right, which could have worse consequences than the duopolistic governance it seeks to overturn. (Macron's new assemblage of the center is a striking counterexample, and much rides on its performance.) In the United States, scholars have identified the causes and consequences of polarization, but the political parties have done nothing to address it. Although candidates and newly elected leaders ritually promise to "bring us together again," polarization has steadily worsened for a generation or more.

There is an obvious cure for excessive concentration of power: a selective devolution of decision-making to subordinate jurisdictions. A quarter century ago, for example, Alice Rivlin proposed a transfer of responsibility for education, infrastructure, and workforce development in return for a federal assumption of full responsibility for health care.[8] But there is a structural clash between dispersing power and the enforcement of common standards across jurisdictions, which both businesses and social activists typically favor. Tensions between centers and peripheries were common in political units as small as Greek city-states, so it may be unreasonable to expect that the larger communities of modern times can do much to temper them. Better performance by the institutions at the center would take the edge off this complaint, which is probably the best that can be done.

Although political corruption varies across place and time, it is as old as organized political society, as are the character flaws it reflects. (Modernity has hardly changed this. The complexity of the modern state multiplies opportunities for self-dealing, but communications technology makes it more transparent once it comes to light.) Nor is cynicism about politicians anything new. Mark Twain famously remarked, "There is no distinctly native American criminal class—except Congress."[9]

"Getting money out of politics" has become a staple of U.S. reform rhetoric, but this will not be possible without major changes in American politics. Long, expensive political campaigns force most politicians to spend inordinate time raising money from people who expect a return on their investment. Shorter contests and ample free television time would relieve much of the pressure, but this is easier said than done. Even harder to imagine are changes in current modes of legislation and regulation that would reduce opportunities for special interests backed by concentrated resources to shape outcomes to their advantage.

But the public's understanding of corruption goes well beyond bribery and the role of money in politics. The heart of the matter, ordinary people believe, is the forms of favoritism in which money is not directly involved. For example: some parents have access to good schools for their children, while others do not. Some groups benefit from public programs from which others feel unjustly excluded. Ethnic identity affects access to college and jobs. A complex tax code benefits those with the resources to hire lawyers and accountants.

This broader conception of corruption helps explain why since 2010 more than seven in ten Americans have consistently said that "corruption is widespread throughout the government in this country."[10] A party that committed itself to the principle of "equal opportunity for all, special privileges for none" would find a broad response across lines that now divide Americans. So would a party that attacked what economists call "rent-seeking": the use by some of self-interested rules to impose costs and extract resources from others.

Average Americans have noticed what recent scholarship has documented: returns on capital are outstripping gains from labor. Global labor markets and the decline of unions have weakened the bargaining position of workers, trends for which there are no easy fixes. A more promising approach is to democratize capital through measures, such as worker ownership of firms, that share the gains more broadly.

In addition, the public should get a return on public capital the benefits of which are now privately appropriated. When the government funds basic research that leads to new medical devices, the firms that have relied on this research should pay royalties to the Treasury. When states and localities invest in infrastructure that raises property values and creates new business opportunities, the taxpayers should receive some portion of the gains. One might even imagine public contributions to a sovereign wealth fund that would invest in an index of U.S. firms and pay dividends to every citizen.

Many people believe that partisan gerrymandering of legislative districts is largely responsible for the hyperpolarization that now disfigures American politics. It is certainly disturbing when politicians pick their voters rather than the other way around. Unfortunately, political scientists have found that partisan line-drawing is responsible for only a modest portion of the rise in polarization.

More significant has been Americans' tendency to sort themselves geographically into like-minded communities. This is why we have so many more counties and even states dominated by one party than we did half a century ago.

Within these single-party zones, political seats are decided by battles within the dominant party rather than between the parties. The system of party primaries, created as a reform during the Progressive Era a century ago, gives disproportionate power to the most intensely mobilized groups within each party, making the compromises essential to effective governance far more difficult. But it is hard to imagine restoring the status quo ante in which candidates were chosen by party regulars in the proverbial "smoke-filled rooms," and not only because the twenty-first-century version would have to be smoke-free.

Reducing public ire at self-dealing depends more on the system's overall performance than on new rules regulating politicians' conduct. If average families are moving ahead, the fact that elected officials and lobbyists are doing well for themselves becomes less salient. But when so many Americans have to work hard just to stay even, it is natural for them to believe that politicians are prospering at their expense. Effective governance may not cure all ills, but it makes these ills easier to bear.

It is easier to invoke the ideal of effectiveness than to produce it. Still, some first steps are clear. Modest changes to federal budget procedures, which have not been reformed since the 1970s, could greatly reduce the threat of government shutdowns and allow departments and agencies to plan with greater confidence. There is no good reason the process by which senior federal officials are nominated and confirmed needs to be as long and tortuous as it has become. Streamlining the U.S. permitting process for major infrastructure projects, now the lengthiest of all the advanced economies, would accelerate job creation and improve economic efficiency without jeopardizing health, safety, and environmental protections.

Some observers want to go farther. In a recent interview, Francis Fukuyama criticized what he called America's "vetocracy," which blocks needed action. "Political decay comes," he asserted, when "interest groups really use their power to veto things not in their interest."[11] This is true, and a modest agenda of reducing veto points makes sense. But the devices that can prevent good things from happening also can prevent bad things from happening. Institutions that can thwart the will of the majority also can prevent undue concentrations of power, which James Madison rightly denounced as the "very definition of tyranny."[12] The government of the United States will regain its capacity to act only when the American people decide to punish the elected officials most responsible for gridlock.

A Cultural Shift

During recent decades, higher education has emerged as a fundamental divide in American society (and in most other Western democracies). Independent of its effect on income, higher education tends to create optimism about the future and openness to change and diversity. As a group, individuals with higher education value science, professional expertise, and relationships across national boundaries. Those without a higher education value these things much less.

In themselves, these differences are not a cause for alarm. But difficulties emerge when educational inequalities become markers of social status. Put bluntly, if Americans with more education regard their less educated fellow citizens with disrespect, the inevitable response from the disrespected will be resentment coupled with a desire to take revenge on those who assert superiority. Much of the populist spirit in the United States reflects this dynamic.

No matter how deeply a society is committed to individuals'

moral equality, social hierarchy is inevitable. But elites have a choice: they can try to take the edge off status differences, or they can flaunt them. Repeated references to flyover country only add insult to the injury of a new economy in which elites' prosperity is increasingly decoupled from the fate of less fortunate parts of American society. It is up to privileged Americans to take the first step by listening attentively and respectfully to those who went unheard for far too long.

Renewed respect for all citizens means taking their views seriously. Most people believe that the nation—their country—is a morally significant community whose interests their leaders should defend. "America First" may be a blunt slogan with ugly historical resonances, but it corresponds to broad public sentiments. The real debate should not be about the priority the interests of one's country should enjoy but rather be about the best understanding of these interests. If those who believe in international engagement cede the terrain of nationalism to populists, they will place themselves permanently on the defensive.

Donald Trump argued, with considerable success, that current arrangements represent unfair bargains by which America transfers resources to other nations without getting equal or greater value in return. Unless internationalists are prepared to defend alliances and transnational institutions as charitable contributions to global well-being, they must meet the populist challenge on its own terms. They must argue that what the United States gains from its alliances, its military deployments, and its defense of freedom of the seas vastly outweighs the cost of maintaining these ventures. And they must frame their argument in terms that appeal to the many Americans who believe that other countries have taken advantage of us for far too long.

As populist movements have surged, a major strategic debate has broken out among populism's foes: Should center-left forces try to regain lost support among working-class voters, or should they look elsewhere for new alliances? Bo Rothstein, a well-known scholar of European social democracy, argues, "The more than 150-year-old alliance between the industrial working class and what one might call the intellectual-cultural Left is over." The reason: "These two now have almost completely different views on key social and political issues." He elaborates: "The traditional working class favours protectionism, the re-establishment of a type of work that the development of technology inexorably has rendered outdated and production over environmental concerns; it is also a significant part of the basis for the recent surge in anti-immigrant and even xenophobic views. Support from the traditional working class for strengthening ethnic or sexual minorities' rights is also pretty low." Because the intellectual-cultural Left is that "exact opposite," Rothstein recommends a new alliance between the left and the "new entrepreneurial economy."[13]

There are counterparts to this argument among center-left leaders in the United States. The best known have based their case on long-cycle demographic shifts. There is a "rising American electorate" made up of educated professionals, minorities, and young people, all groups whose share of the electorate will increase steadily over the next two generations. These groups represent the future. The white working class, whose electoral share has dwindled in recent decades and will continue to do so, is the past.[14] This does not mean that the center-left should ignore it completely. It does mean that there should be no compromise with white working-class sentiments on the social and cultural issues that dominate the concerns of the rising American electorate coalition. This was the theory at the heart of Hillary Clinton's presidential campaign.

If concessions on cultural and social issues are ruled out, appeals to the white working class will have to be confined to economics. This is the line that "progressives" now advocate, and it shaped Senator Bernie Sanders's insurgent campaign as well as the revamped economic agenda unveiled by Democratic leaders in mid-2017. The difficulty, as we have seen, is that the audience for this economic appeal cares at least as much about social and cultural issues. Immigration, demographic change, and fears of cultural displacement drove the Brexit vote, and they were the key determinants of Donald Trump's victory. Although Jeremy Corbyn's Labour Party, which waged a classic campaign focused on the economy and social services, did better than expected in the 2017 British general election, it did not come close to winning.

So the American center-left has a choice: to stand firm on social and cultural issues that antagonize populism's most fervent supporters, or to shift in ways for which it can offer a principled defense. It is time for an open and robust debate on issues of immigration, identity politics, and nationalism that liberals and progressives have long avoided.

SEVEN

Democratic Leadership

As the contemporary challenge to liberal democracy has escalated, political observers have distinguished between two unsatisfactory responses—the "illiberal democracy" of Hungary's Viktor Orban and his acolytes and the "undemocratic liberalism" of experts, courts, and international bureaucracies. This up-to-the-minute analysis has deep historical roots. Throughout history, democracies have struggled against both populism and elitism, often in the form of individuals who present themselves as potential leaders.

Political communities need good leaders, but not all forms of political organization are equally hospitable to the leadership they need. There is a perennial worry that democracy and leadership are fundamentally at odds. While there is no contradiction between leadership and democratic principles, there is certainly a tension between leadership and democratic psychology. Some of this tension is productive, but much is not. Taken too far, the passions and emotions characteristic of democracy can end by weakening it.

We may wonder whether the excellences of leadership are everywhere and always the same. In *Politics* (III.4), Aristotle famously argues that the virtues of citizens are relative to the regime, by which he means that good citizens are not necessarily good human beings. What about leaders? Aristotle seems to suggest that the virtues of good rulers are the same as the virtues of good men, which are the same in all times and circumstances. If that were so, there would be nothing distinctive about democratic leadership.

But the matter is more complicated. Aristotle grounds politics in the human capacity for speech (I.2), and he goes on to argue that political leadership is qualitatively different from other kinds of rule in that it is governance "over free and equal persons" (I.7).[1] Politics involves a relationship among human beings who are not in principle rightly subject to either coercion or command. The core of political rule is persuasion—the ability to induce agreement about what should be done. On the eve of Dwight Eisenhower's inauguration, outgoing president Harry Truman is said to have remarked, "[Ike] will say, 'Do this! Do that!' and nothing will happen. Poor Ike—it won't be a bit like the army."[2] Although Truman failed to grasp how much of the success Eisenhower earned as supreme commander of the allied forces had rested on his powers of persuasion, he was right about the underlying principle: the essence of politics is coordination of wills through persuasion rather than through unquestioning obedience.

Whether good leadership is always and everywhere the same depends on whether the capacity for persuasion is the same in all political circumstances. To clarify this issue, we can turn to *Rhetoric*, in which Aristotle identifies three sources of persuasion—character, emotion, and argument. All three relate in different ways to the political context in which one is operating.

In the first place, certain character traits will commend speakers to their audience in some contexts but not others. As Aristotle puts it, "We ought to be acquainted with the characters of each form of government; for in reference to each, the character most likely to persuade must be that which is characteristic of it" (I.8).[3] While certain traits—such as probity in financial matters and devotion to the common good—are universally prized, others are more regime specific. They promote a regime's distinctive ends. If the end of democracy is liberty, then democratic citizens will prize traits seen as defending liberty. (From this perspective, it would be hard to improve on "Give me liberty or give me death.") Other traits reflect and honor a regime's core beliefs. If equal opportunity and upward mobility are prized, as they are in the United States, then someone who started with nothing and "worked her way up" will be regarded as possessing admirable traits of character—grit and determination, among others. As American history repeatedly shows, these traits commend themselves to democratic electorates and to their representatives. (No doubt Sonia Sotomayor's inspiring rise from poverty eased her confirmation as the first Hispanic Supreme Court justice.)

Similarly, some emotions are more characteristic of democratic polities than others. For example, people who prize liberty tend to be on their guard against those who might deprive them of it, and those who wield power are in a position to do that. So democracy and suspicion of authority tend to go together. Another example: if the equal freedom of democratic citizens leads them to regard themselves as possessing equal worth and merit, then they will resent individuals seen as giving themselves airs—those whom they see as claiming to be better than others. Populist resentment is an enduring staple of democratic politics. To avoid resentment, democratic leaders from wealthy families must display an unfeigned common touch. Franklin Roosevelt once served hot dogs to the king and queen of England at a Hyde Park picnic, an event the *New York Times* treated as front-page news.[4]

A third example: as Plato was perhaps the first to observe, the democratic preference for liberty tends to generate a certain tolerance of varying ways of life. The desire to live just as one pleases softens antipathy to those who live differently but do not impede one's own choices. "Live and let live" is a perennial democratic sentiment.

Finally, the premises that are generally accepted as bases of public argument will vary with the political context. For example, claims erected on the foundation of individual rights are more powerful in the United States than in most other nations—even other advanced democracies. Each country possesses a distinctive public culture: a set of beliefs that amalgamate principle, shared history, and distinctive ethnicities.

Leadership Is Consistent with Democratic Principles but Not with Democratic Psychology

Is there a fundamental tension between leadership and the democratic principle of popular sovereignty? In a pathbreaking book, John Kane and Haig Patapan argue that there is. The principle of equality, on which democracy rests, "affords democrats no completely satisfying way of justifying leadership roles." Supporters of democracy who believe in the necessity of leadership "must reconcile this with the belief that none among equals has any *innate* or *inherent* right to rule over others."[5]

The Kane-Patapan thesis rests on an implied syllogism that runs like this:

Premise 1: The justification of leadership requires the belief that some individuals have an innate or inherent right to rule over others.
Premise 2: Principled democrats must reject the idea that anyone has such a right.
Conclusion: Democrats who understand their creed must

believe that leadership cannot be justified in principle. To the extent that democrats feel the need for leadership in practice, they run up against a fundamental tension that can be managed but never eliminated.

Clearly, the second premise states a basic democratic commitment. But the syllogism fails because neither democratic principles nor the nature of leadership require us to accept the first premise. Democrats can embrace leadership as legitimate when it comes into being through popular authorization, and as appropriate when it serves democratic purposes. A democratic people can constitute leadership for instrumental reasons—because certain individuals have the capacities that the situation requires—without affirming that those individuals have a right to rule, simply by virtue of those capacities. Not even the singularly ideal person to lead a democracy has the right to lead it, unless the people have vested him or her with the power to do so. In democracies, the capacity to lead does not by itself confer a right to lead.

There may of course be prudential reasons for preferring some individuals over others to fill specific positions. Just as we seek a skilled plumber to fix a faucet, we want able generals to conduct a war and superior politicians to shape policy, because they know how to do something that promotes our good, as we understand it. The people would be wise, then, to choose the ablest politicians as their leaders, and their leaders would be wise to select the best generals to command their forces. But in a democracy, generals do not legitimately lead unless the people's representatives have authorized them to do so. Individual ability is relevant, but legitimacy is dispositive, and democratic legitimacy comes only through public consent.

The people's representatives may err, of course. President Lincoln promoted and then dismissed many generals before finding a few who could get the job done. Army chief of staff George C.

Marshall did the same thing during World War II. The people have the right to make mistakes, but only their decisions can confer legitimacy.

There is no essential conflict between democratic equality and leadership. Moral equality—the idea that my interests count no more and no less than yours—is consistent with inequality of talents in every walk of life, including politics. Moral equality is the basis of popular sovereignty, which James Madison called the republican principle—a form of government that "derives all its powers directly or indirectly from the great body of the people."⁶ This principle is the core of republican legitimacy. Consistent with legitimacy so understood, the people may authorize whatever institutions they choose, including institutions of leadership, and they may revise or revoke such authorization as they see fit.

That said, well-designed democratic institutions endeavor to narrow the gap between the authorization to lead and capacity to do it well. Elections may be understood as an example of this effort. While they reflect the public's will, they are also designed to select individuals with the requisite talent and character to discharge the duties of public office. As Aristotle observed, a lottery is the most purely democratic means of selecting public officials, while elections have an aristocratic tendency (*Politics* IV.9).

Members of America's founding generation were well aware of this tendency, and they celebrated it. Defending the proposed constitution's means of selecting the president, Alexander Hamilton declared in *Federalist* No. 68 that it would afford a "moral certainty" that the office would seldom fall to any man "who is not in an eminent degree endowed with the requisite qualifications." Indeed, he continued, "there will be a constant probability of seeing the station filled by characters preeminent for ability and virtue."⁷ In a letter to John Adams, Thomas Jefferson wrote: "There is a natural aristocracy among men. The grounds of this are virtue and talents.

. . . May we not even say that that form of government is best, which provides the most effectually for a pure selection of these natural *aristoi* into the offices of government?" This, he argued, was the genius of our constitutional order, "to leave to the citizens the free election and separation of the *aristoi* from the *pseudo-aristoi*, the separation of the wheat from the chaff." Most of the time, we can rely on the people to make discriminating judgments, to "elect the really good and wise."[8]

To be sure, episodes throughout history have challenged the founders' confidence in elections as reliable sorting mechanisms. Some presidents, such as James Buchanan and Herbert Hoover, failed to meet the challenge of their times. Many Americans believe that Donald Trump lacks the knowledge and temperament that every president needs. From time to time in the life of every individual, passion overwhelms reason and judgment, and so too for peoples. Although well-designed institutions can reduce the odds of damaging mistakes, they cannot eliminate the possibility that voters in their least wise and moderate moments will act in ways that undermine their own interests and those of the country.

Are there any democratic alternatives to elections? Although selecting leaders by lottery is consistent with antielitist sentiments, I am unaware of any modern democracy that has used this procedure for any significant office. William F. Buckley Jr. once remarked that he would rather be governed by the first two thousand people listed in the Boston telephone directory than by the Harvard faculty, but this was a judgment on the deficiencies of Harvard.[9] Some small towns have resorted to randomizing devices such as coin tosses to break tie votes for local offices, but invariably not much is at stake in such choices. The people recognize that elections allow them to make comparative judgments about qualifications for office. The candidates may be equal in the sight of God and the law yet differ in their capacity to fill positions of responsibility.

The Populist Challenge to Democratic Leadership

Leadership comes into conflict not with the principle of democracy but with its psychology. One aspect of this psychology is populism, a complex of sentiments and beliefs that includes the following:

- *leveling*—the belief that common sense trumps expertise and that ordinary citizens are better suited than experts to make decisions;
- *animus against hierarchy*—an instinctive bridling against taking orders from anyone;
- *suspicion of power* as inherently corrupt and self-dealing;
- *mistrust of distance* between the people and those chosen to represent them, and a desire for officials they can see and judge directly;
- *mistrust of anything less than full transparency;* and
- *the demand for constant,* as opposed to episodic, *explanation and accountability.*

Kane and Patapan are right to see these sentiments as at odds with the exercise of leadership. Carried too far, they are at odds with the people's own interests, as they themselves understand them. (For example, Venezuela's populist regime began by giving the people the economic and social programs they said they wanted, and ended by plunging the country into hyperinflation, deep recession, and widespread hunger.) Kane and Patapan are also right to point out the difference between the classical conception of democracy and modern liberalism. The latter contains principled limits to the scope of public power, and suspicion focuses primarily on the threats to liberty that emerge when government overreaches. In the classical conception of democracy, the focus is not on the scope of public power but rather on hierarchical relations among citizens. As the authors put it, "Democracy is at root a revolt against the rank ordering of society. . . . The leveling instinct of democracy is principally directed against the arrogance of inherited or entrenched power."[10]

As a liberal democracy, governance in America incurs populist suspicion of both forms of arrogance. The people resent individuals who visibly regard themselves as superior to their fellow citizens and they also fear government that expands its power in a way that threatens liberty. During the Obama administration, these two populisms merged: opponents of the administration saw a dangerous growth in the scope of government, driven by the belief that a handful of elected or appointed officials could make better decisions for the people than the people could make for themselves. (For opponents of Obama's health care reform, the boards of experts it established and empowered represented the distilled essence of this mindset.)

This stance represents perennial American populism, the sentiment that prevails during normal times, as distinguished from the variant that arises in response to perceived threats, when fear sparks the yearning for strong leadership. This perennial populism reflects America's traditional suspicion of government power. Much of this suspicion is a by-product of representation, which is the only way democracy can function at all under what Madison called the extended republic. To be sure, there is more than one kind of representation. The Burkean view—the representative as trustee who pursues the common good as he or she sees it—is greatly admired in theory but avoided in practice. In contemporary democracies, voters can see what their representatives are doing, and they have limited tolerance for independent judgment. At the other extreme, voters are bound to be frustrated if they expect representatives identical to themselves. Democratic legislators must deal with myriad issues about which their constituents know little or nothing, and they must balance competing loyalties to their electorate, their party, and their country.

We are left with an inescapable social reality: whenever the people do not rule themselves directly, some individuals (agents) are asked to carry out the wishes of others (principals). But there is an extensive literature exploring how the interests of agents and principals diverge. Citizens would be foolish to assume that their representatives will advance their interests just because they have been sent to Washington and state capitals to do so.

There is a second pervasive fact that gives rise to suspicion: it is impossible to write laws, regulations, and rules to cover every eventuality. Thus no government can do without discretionary authority. Democracies use statutes and regulatory procedures to delimit the sphere of authorized discretion before the fact, and legislative oversight and elections to judge its use after the fact. They cannot hope to eliminate discretion altogether.

That unattainable desire, however, drives much of contemporary American politics. The understandable wish to ensure that no one is subject to the arbitrary will of another gives rise to an ever more elaborate system of rules, regulations, and review procedures. The result is not to eliminate discretion but to tie major institutions in knots, making them less and less able to make needed judgments and to do the people's business. Americans' fear of discretionary authority fuels the endless expansion of the bureaucracy they despise.

Up to a point, perennial populism has its uses. As Kane and Patapan observe, mistrust of leadership constitutes a barrier against tyranny, supplementing constitutional restraints. But so understood, populism often overshoots this mark, weakening the leaders and institutions needed to effectuate the people's choices and promote the people's welfare. Kane and Patapan adduce a remarkable quote from Henry Clay: "The pervading principle of our system of government—of all free government—is not merely the possibility, but the absolute certainty of infidelity and treachery."[11] Clay was a great leader, but he went far beyond the nuanced views of James Madison, who argued in *Federalist* No. 55: "As there is a degree of depravity in mankind which requires a certain degree of circumspection and distrust, so there are other qualities in human nature which justify a certain portion of esteem and confidence. Republican government presupposes the existence of these qualities in a higher degree than any other form. Were the pictures which have been drawn by the political jealousy of some among us faithful likenesses of the human character, the inference would be that there is not sufficient virtue among us for self-government."[12]

This balanced judgment illuminates the difference between proper democratic caution and the populist culture of suspicion. Fear of corruption and tyranny can go so far as to undermine self-government. The point of democratic elections is to find people worthy of the people's trust. When the people succumb to unalloyed mistrust, democracy loses its capacity to serve their interests.

The Elitist Challenge to Good Democratic Leadership

The experience of democratic life can produce a stance diametrically opposed to populist resentment—namely, elitist arrogance. It is natural for people of unusual ability to believe that their merits entitle them to positions of leadership, and to a measure of deference. They may ask themselves why those of lesser merit should be able to confer or withhold what belongs by right to those with greater capacities, and they may come to feel thwarted and demeaned by the processes of popular consent.

Shakespeare presents us with a perfect example of such a man. Returning in triumph after his victory over the Volscians, the Roman nobleman and warrior Coriolanus is on the verge of being named consul. Once the Senate has given its consent, custom demands that the candidate present himself to the commoners and request their support. When he meets the people, they ask him why he has come. "Mine own desert," he replies. The people are astonished and displeased; this is not the supplication they expected. Coriolanus then asks them the price of the consulship. "The price is, to ask it kindly," replies one. The proud Coriolanus utters—but almost chokes on—the required words. After the citizens have taken their leave, he bursts forth in an angry soliloquy: "Better it is to die, better to starve, than crave the hire which first we do deserve" (*Coriolanus*, II.iii).[13] As the play reveals, this passion is a threat to civic order.

General Douglas MacArthur may have been the American Coriolanus. A gifted and charismatic military leader and statesman who orchestrated Japan's immediate postwar reconstruction, MacArthur's belief in his own merits led him to challenge the principle of civilian control over the military. At the height of the Korean War, he sent a letter to the House minority leader disagreeing with President Truman's effort to avoid a wider war with China, and his public statements undermined Truman's diplomacy. In April 1951, Truman relieved him of command, replacing him with General Matthew Ridgway, who knew MacArthur as well as anyone did. Ridgway professed the deepest respect for his predecessor's "abilities, for his courage and for his tactical brilliance . . . for his leadership, his quick mind and his unusual skill at going straight to the point of any subject and illuminating it. . . . He was . . . a truly great military man, a great statesman, and a gallant leader." But Ridgway also noted MacArthur's "tendency to cultivate the isolation that genius seems to require, until it became a sort of insulation . . . ; the headstrong quality . . . that sometimes led him to persist in a cause in defiance of all logic; [and] a faith in his own judgment . . . that finally led him close to insubordination." If MacArthur had pursued the presidency, as he was widely expected to do in 1952 after his triumphant return to the United States, these qualities could have posed a threat to the constitutional order.[14]

One might think that while populist resentment is a deformation internal to democracy, overweening elitism is an external threat. But matters are not so simple. There is often a tension between government by the people and government for the people. While the people always desire their well-being, they are not always clear —or even coherent—about the means to that end. Talented and public-spirited individuals who genuinely want to promote the public interest can end up longing for leadership that is not regularly accountable to the people. The mirror image of the populism that disfigures today's politics in America is a growing doubt, expressed more in private than in public, about the people's capacity to govern themselves—especially when they are asked to endure short-term pain as the price of long-term gain.

The Skills and Virtues of Good Democratic Leaders
Good democratic leaders combine capability and legitimacy: they have the attributes needed to exercise power wisely while respecting the ongoing need for public authorization. This distinctive ensemble helps us understand the specific skills and virtues of democratic leaders.

Good democratic leadership requires the specific skills needed to obtain and sustain public support. To begin with, democratic leaders must understand and be able to articulate the public culture of their community. In so doing, they invite the people to unite around the fundamentals of their civic identity. Martin Luther King Jr.'s "I Have a Dream" speech, which drew on America's biblical and constitutional heritage, was a classic of that genre. So were Franklin Roosevelt's "Four Freedoms" address and, in a different vein, Ronald Reagan's acceptance speech at the 1980 Republican convention. Reagan summoned up the Mayflower Compact, the signers of the Declaration of Independence, Abraham Lincoln, FDR, and even Thomas Paine. Invoking "family, work, neighborhood, peace and freedom," he implored the American people to "renew our compact of freedom . . . for the sake of this, our beloved and blessed land." He defined this "new beginning" as a commitment to "care for the needy; to teach our children the values and virtues handed down to us by our families; to have the courage to defend those values and the willingness to sacrifice for them [and] to restore, in our time, the American spirit of voluntary service, of cooperation, of private and community initiative, a spirit that flows like a deep and mighty river through the history of our nation."[15] His deep patriotism impressed even those Reagan did not persuade and helped lay the foundation for an effective presidency.

Another key requirement of democratic leadership is the capacity to understand what is required in particular circumstances to maximize persuasion and popular consent. Earl Warren displayed this capacity in the months leading up to the Supreme Court's 1954 decision in *Brown v. Board of Education*. By 1952, five major school segregation cases had reached the Court, which decided to hear them collectively. The justices soon realized that they were badly divided. Unable to reach a resolution by the end of the 1952–53 term, they decided to rehear the case in December 1953. In the interim, Chief Justice Fred Vinson died, and Governor Earl Warren of California was confirmed as his replacement. Warren quickly concluded that unless the Court were united, a decision declaring school segregation unconstitutional would not achieve the requisite degree of public acceptance. Over the next six months, he worked patiently to bring about that result, adopting Justice Robert Jackson's recommendation to delay taking formal votes until the issues had been thoroughly debated. This process enabled the justices to identify grounds for judgment on which all could agree. On May 14, 1954, the chief justice was able to announce a unanimous decision outlawing school segregation.[16]

This is not to say that *Brown v. Board of Education* evoked the same unity among the American people. Its legitimacy was bitterly contested, especially but not only in the South, inspiring the "Impeach Earl Warren" bumper stickers that festooned so many cars. Nonetheless, the judgment of most historians is that the Court's unanimity added moral force to its decision. The ruling brought together nine justices with very different backgrounds, views, and jurisprudential tendencies. The Court spoke in the name of the nation, not an ideological faction, and its voice enjoyed a greater degree of trust and deference than it would otherwise have received. We will never know, of course, what would have happened if the case had been decided by a 5–4 margin. Still, Warren's achievement stands as an example of democratic leadership in action.

Timing is vital to successful leadership. Act too early, and conditions are not ripe; too late, and the momentum has ebbed. As Brutus famously proclaimed in *Julius Caesar* (IV.iii), "There is a tide in the affairs of men which, taken at the flood, leads on to fortune; omitted, all the voyage of their life is bound in shallows and in miseries."[17] Knowing which way the tide is running, and whether it is strong enough, is one of the most difficult judgments for any leader to make.

This was the question Abraham Lincoln faced as he wrestled with the timing of the Emancipation Proclamation. Abolitionists were pressuring him to free all the slaves, while Northern Democrats and the loyal border states pushed hard in the other direction. The available evidence suggested that a majority of the public was opposed to emancipation. On the other hand, the longer Lincoln waited, the greater the chance that Britain and France would recognize the Confederacy, dealing a severe blow to Union prospects. To complicate matters further, he believed he had no peacetime authority under the Constitution to end slavery. Emancipation could be justified (if at all) only as an exercise of his powers as commander in chief. But resting his case on military necessity meant that slaves could be freed only in states (or portions of states) under Confederate control. So conceived, the Emancipation Proclamation would free slaves over whom he did not exercise control, while leaving those he did control in servitude—an irony his Abolitionist critics repeatedly underscored.

Lincoln navigated carefully through these shoals. He began by discussing the matter with his cabinet in the summer of 1862, arguing that the Proclamation had to be seen as an act of strength rather than desperation. Union successes at Antietam met that condition, enabling Lincoln to move forward in two stages. In September 1862, he announced his intention to emancipate the slaves in all areas of the Confederacy not under Union control as of January 1, 1863. As he feared, even this modest first step sparked a fierce political reaction and became a campaign issue. Opposition Democrats gained twenty-eight House seats in the midterm election of 1862, as well as the governorship of New York—a serious reversal, but not a death knell for congressional Republicans or the Lincoln administration. The Proclamation itself, issued as promised on January 1, 1863, not only shored up Lincoln's standing among radical Republicans but also persuaded Britain and France, both of which had already abolished slavery, not to recognize the Confederacy—a major turning point in the war.[18]

In retrospect, it appears Lincoln's timing was correct. If Lincoln had moved more precipitately, the negative response would probably have been even greater, and opposition Democrats might have gained enough power in the 1862 election to challenge Republican war policies. If he had waited much longer, recognition by France and Britain could have strengthened the South enough to produce a long stalemate and rising support for peace talks in the North. As it was, the Democrats drafted a platform calling for an immediate cease-fire, and Lincoln's reelection victory over George McClellan hung in the balance until the fall of 1864, when Union military successes shifted public opinion in his favor.

In addition to skills, democratic leadership requires a strong set of virtues to safeguard it from going astray. One such virtue is what I call democratic humility: the belief that the legitimacy of your power ultimately depends on the will of the people, not just on your own merit. It is easier to state this proposition than to practice it. During the confirmation process for senior positions in the executive branch and the judiciary, even the most outstanding nominees are instructed to flatter the people's representatives, to answer—gravely and respectfully—even their most uninformed questions, and to treat even their most trivial utterances as timeless aphorisms. Candidates for high elective office find themselves pressured to evade what they know to be the real choices and to make promises they know they cannot keep. Many officials privately believe—even if they will not publicly admit—that sound public policy requires substantial insulation from public scrutiny. Lincoln thought that only a carefully cultivated reverence for the Constitution—and the principle of human equality at its base—could save us from antidemocratic sentiments. Madison believed that the chastening effects of elections—the requirement to seek public authorization—would habituate us to respect republican norms.[19] Both understood the centrality of democratic humility to the kind of leadership that preserves and strengthens self-government.

The tension between leadership and democratic humility comes to a head in moments of civic danger. Statesmanship is a particular kind of leadership displayed in particular circumstances. It is an ensemble of qualities that enable its possessors to preserve regimes against profound challenges or to improve them in fundamental ways. Times that call only for routine governance do not permit the exercise of statesmanship, which can be displayed only in extreme situations—founding, war, economic collapse, deep civic division. Ambitious leaders in tranquil times (Bill Clinton, for one) sometimes yearn for less orderly circumstances in which they can distinguish themselves. But if leaders prove unequal to such circumstances, as did James Buchanan in the 1850s and Neville Chamberlain in the 1930s, they only win ignominy.

Democratic peoples—especially Americans—respond strongly to moral narratives that cleanly distinguish between the forces of good and evil. They have a harder time coming to grips with moral complexity and ambiguity. Private and public morality sometimes diverge. The norms of foreign policy and war are not congruent with those of domestic affairs. And the virtues of the private household do not always map neatly onto those of the public household. For example, most economists believe that poorly timed public thrift—austerity—can make a bad economic situation worse. But most people have a hard time understanding why it can be right for a government to spend more than it is taking in—especially if the public deficit is used to finance current consumption. While many parents grasp the rationale of going into debt to finance a college education, they are loath to cosign loans for children's fancy cars and flat-screen TVs.

President Obama faced—or thought he faced—this kind of problem early in his administration. The Great Recession generated pressure to humiliate and punish the financial leaders the people held responsible for the housing collapse. In the administration's view, this demand raised two problems. First, responsibility for the financial meltdown was broadly shared among many institutions and individuals (including improvident borrowers as well as reckless lenders). Second, with the global financial system tottering, a frontal attack on financial leaders could bring a complete collapse. So the administration shored up the banks, incurring the public's wrath. Few financial leaders faced trial, and none of any significance went to jail. The clash between the moral narrative and the perceived imperatives of public policy could not have been sharper. (Political pundits and policy experts continue to debate the accuracy of President Obama's assessment.)

The Ultimate Test of Democratic Leadership

The last, most needed, most paradoxical attribute of democratic leadership is the willingness to forgo power when attaining and maintaining it requires morally unacceptable compromise. Democratic politics at its best is the use of publicly authorized power to advance the common good. Would-be leaders, then, can fail in two ways: they may be unable to obtain public support for their agenda, or they may win support by advocating only what the people want to hear. While modern survey research has raised the assessment of public beliefs to a high art, the temptation to pander to them is a perennial weakness of democratic politics.

On the other hand, principled aspirants cannot hope to win power by bluntly saying exactly what they believe. For example, while his desire to support Britain's struggle against Nazi Germany was completely justified, FDR might well have lost his 1940 re-election campaign if he had been completely candid about it. So he equivocated. When Wendell Willkie, the Republican presidential nominee, claimed that a vote for Roosevelt meant war in 1941, Roosevelt countered with a flat promise to the contrary—"Your boys are not going to be sent into any foreign wars"—deliberately omitting the Democratic platform's qualifying phrase, "except in case of attack." When one of his speechwriters asked about the omission, he replied, "Of course we'll fight if we're attacked. If someone attacks us, then it isn't a foreign war, is it?"[20] This mental reservation allowed Roosevelt to pretend that he wasn't trying to mislead the people, which of course he was.

On a deeper level, though, one can offer a moral as well as democratic defense of Roosevelt's strategy. FDR knew that Americans would fight if attacked, even if they would turn against someone who said so in advance of the attack, and he believed that he was the best man to lead America in the war he considered inevitable. So he stayed as close to the truth as democratic politics would permit. Still, campaign utterances have consequences. What many heard as a promise to keep the United States out of war made it more difficult for FDR to mobilize public support for the lend-lease program, without which Britain might have collapsed before Pearl Harbor brought America into the war.

Although Franklin Roosevelt was a man of sincere convictions, it is not clear what political risks he was willing to run in their defense. John McCain, by contrast, was willing to jeopardize his career to adhere to his principles. Frustrated by his primary defeat to George W. Bush in 2000, his desire to run and win in 2008 was palpable. At the same time, he believed that the national interest required a new approach to immigration policy. This stance greatly dismayed most Republicans, in and out of Congress. McCain, who had begun his quest for his party's nomination as the frontrunner, found that his support had all but evaporated by the summer of 2007. His lonely but successful effort to revive his candidacy is one of the most remarkable chapters in the annals of modern American politics.

These episodes suggest that Plato's judgment of democratic publics was too harsh. True, the people do not welcome being told what they do not want to hear. At the same time, they admire individuals who come before them with strong convictions about their community's best interests. Candor fosters trust, and a reputation for trustworthiness is one of the most valuable assets a democratic politician can acquire.

Because many Americans regarded Hillary Clinton as deficient in candor, they did not trust her, and their mistrust overwhelmed the appeal of her knowledge and experience. Conversely, those who supported Donald Trump saw him as a man of strong convictions who would say what he believed, regardless of the consequences, and this tendency more than counterbalanced statements and attributes that would have disqualified any other candidate. The chaotic early months of Trump's presidency led even members of his own party to wonder whether the American people got it right.

Extracts are from pp. 15–31, chapter 2, "Populist Resentment, Elitist Arrogance: Two Challenges to Good Democratic Leadership" by William A. Galston, from *Good Democratic Leadership: On Prudence and Judgment in Modern Democracies*, edited by John Kane and Haig Patapan. © the several contributors 2014. By permission of Oxford University Press.

EIGHT

The Incompleteness of Liberal Democracy

In everyday modern parlance, "populism" stands for a particular brand of politics: the rising up of the common people against those they regard as wielding excessive political, economic, and cultural power. It typically brings to the fore a strong leader who can both channel the sentiments of the public and lead its fight against concentrated power. Populist leaders attack the "enemies of the people" in moralistic terms, as self-seeking, corrupt, and given to conspiracies against ordinary citizens, which often involve hidden links with power holders in other countries. Populism requires constant conflict with these enemies and endless struggle against the forces they represent. Its programs draw bright lines that invite even more conflict: they are nationalist rather than internationalist, and protectionist in the broad sense of the term, serving as bulwarks against foreign goods, foreign immigrants, and foreign ideas.

The populist vision is dyadic. Society is divided into two opposing forces, each of which is internally homogeneous, with a common interest and unitary will. One of these forces (the "people") is completely virtuous: the other (the powerful or the "elite") is irredeemably malign. The evil force is the active agent, working against the interests of its victim, the good force. Because the good are not powerful enough to overcome the forces of darkness, they need a strong leader to defend them against the evil that oppresses them and deprives them of their due.

Although populist movements sometimes erode or even overturn democratic regimes, they are not necessarily antidemocratic. But populism is always anti-pluralist. In this key respect, it represents a challenge to liberal democracy, which stands or falls with the recognition and protection of pluralism.

This challenge exists on a broad front—not only to the failures of liberal democracy but also to its most honorable features. Liberal democracy goes hand in hand with rationalism—respect for science, technical expertise, and evidence-based deliberation—and also with individualism, which combines the blessings of liberty with the burdens of personal responsibility. It requires respect for the rule of law and patience in the making of law.

Citizens of liberal democracies must accept, along with the many advantages of representation, its intrinsic shortcomings. They must acknowledge the necessity of compromise with those with whom they disagree, which is much easier when the matters at issue are material interests rather than differences of principle. They must somehow tolerate, without necessarily admiring, not only deep differences of outlook but also the public expression of these differences, even when they dislike the speech and conduct to which they give rise. Human beings have an ingrained impulse to repress what is disagreeable; refusing to do so is one of the hardest-won victories of liberal character formation.

Liberals are slow to impute absolute evil to their adversaries or all virtue to their friends. They are antitribal, acknowledging particular identities but subordinating them to broader conceptions of civic and even human fellowship. The liberal ethos is resolutely nonheroic, prizing security over risk and peace over war—which is not to say that risk and war can ever be expunged from the life of any society, or that some members of liberal societies will not prize risk-taking or the military life. But as a whole, liberal regimes work hard to afford their citizens as much security as circumstances permit, and they regard war as a disagreeable necessity rather than a glorious adventure.

Liberal democracy presupposes, and to some extent nurtures, a distinctive outlook and political psychology. Many of its requirements are demanding and need a measure of self-restraint. This is a permanent source of vulnerability. Citizens often crave more unity and solidarity than liberal life typically offers, and community can be a satisfying alternative to the burdens of individual responsibility. Preferring those who are most like us goes with the grain of our sentiments more than does a wider, more abstract concept of equal citizenship or humanity. So does the tendency to impute good motives to our friends and malign intent to our foes. Antipathy has its satisfactions, and conflict, like love, can make us feel more fully alive. Populism's embrace of tribalism, its Manichean outlook, and the constant conflict it entails all draw strength from the enduring incompleteness of life in liberal societies.

Passion and Conflict in Liberal Societies

Like the modes of self-interest, passions are facts—part of the basic structure of the human condition. This reality has not always been acknowledged. Since the beginning of modernity, influential thinkers have hoped that self-interest could subdue or even supplant the passions. In 1914, many observers considered a European war unthinkable because of the economic damage it would wreak. As late as 1936, with the horrors of the Great War still fresh, John Maynard Keynes could write: "Dangerous human proclivities can be canalized into comparatively harmless channels by the existence of opportunities for money-making and private wealth, which, if they cannot be satisfied in this way, may find their outlet in cruelty, the reckless pursuit of personal power and authority, and other forms of self-aggrandizement."[1] He seemed to have forgotten that the century of relative peace and prosperity after the Congress of Vienna also witnessed the flowering of antibourgeois sentiments—in particular, contempt for commercial activities and for the self-protective timidity of bourgeois life. The famous words of Rupert Brooke's "Peace," written at the outset of the Great War, reflect this contempt:

> Now, God be thanked Who has matched us with His hour,
> And caught our youth, and wakened us from sleeping,
> With hand made sure, clear eye, and sharpened power,
> To turn, as swimmers into cleanness leaping,
> Glad from a world grown old and cold and weary,
> Leave the sick hearts that honour could not move,
> And half-men, and their dirty songs and dreary,
> And all the little emptiness of love!

These sentiments cannot justify the war, but they help explain it. Even after Brooke's heroic romanticism had given way to the harsh realism of Wilfred Owen's "Dulce et Decorum Est," antibourgeois thinkers and politicians dominated the interwar years, preparing the way for Fascism and National Socialism. In times of chaos and strife, human beings crave the tranquillity of daily life, and many are satisfied when they get it. But some are not, and they tend to include not only the potential leaders of their societies but also individuals whose aspirations extend beyond material comfort. Theories of politics that neglect this dimension of the human condition are bound to be descriptively and normatively inadequate. Realism demands more than a narrow focus on the political order within which individuals can pursue their self-interest.

Discontent with bourgeois life has a long and surprising history, even among noted liberal thinkers. Discussing the defects of a society devoted to market transactions, Adam Smith remarked that commerce "sinks the courage of mankind and tends to extinguish martial spirit." When national defense is consigned to a narrow class of professional warriors, the people grow "effeminate." Worse, their minds are "contracted, and rendered incapable of elevation," and the "heroic spirit . . . is almost lost."[2] In a similar vein, Alexis de Tocqueville once remarked: "War almost always enlarges the mind of a people and raises their character."[3]

We may wonder whether empirical sociology would vindicate these judgments. But their influence on centuries of thinkers and social elites is beyond question. When Brooke denounced the "sick hearts that honour could not move" and welcomed war as "cleanness," he drew on the tradition that juxtaposes the martial virtues to the alleged small-mindedness of daily economic and social life.[4] So did William Butler Yeats in "September 1913" when he condemned people who

> fumble in a greasy till
And add the halfpence to the pence
And prayer to shivering prayer.[5]

Liberal democracy rests on a philosophy of comfortable self-preservation. No doubt this is a pervasive desire, never more than in times of poverty, war, or civil strife. But as strife invites its own antithesis, so does tranquillity. "The impulse to danger and adventure is deeply ingrained in human nature," Bertrand Russell once said, "and no society which ignores it can long be stable."[6] This proposition led William James to search for "a moral equivalent of war." There is no such thing, of course, but political combat comes close. So do social movements, when masses of like-minded individuals find common purpose in the struggle against society's imperfections and injustices. Similar are rare moments of national purpose when charismatic leaders—Franklin D. Roosevelt, John F. Kennedy, Ronald Reagan—inspire high-minded young people to set aside gain in favor of service.

The Ambivalences of Freedom and Equality

Liberal democracy rests too on a philosophy of individual freedom, and with it personal responsibility, but individualism is not always satisfying. Most people crave a measure of community and solidarity that life in individualistic societies often frustrates. The Preamble to the U.S. Constitution speaks of the "blessings of liberty," but freedom can also be a burden. As Erich Fromm argued in *Escape from Freedom*, the anxiety it often produces can lead to the desire to dominate, even destroy, what seems uncontrollable. It can also induce people to seek psychic security through submission to external authority.[7]

Domination and submission are the yin and yang of authoritarianism and also, somewhat more benignly, of hierarchical institutions. As Ernst Junger once said of army life, "Everything is simple. My rights and duties are prescribed. My food is provided, and if things go badly I have a thousand fellow-sufferers. Above all, the shadow of death reduces every problem to a satisfying triviality."[8]

Liberal democracy is poised uneasily between particularism and universalism. On one hand, the commitment to equality erodes distinctions. If dignity and rights pertain to all human beings by virtue of their common humanity, then treating individuals differently based on where they were born or what they revere seems unjustifiable. Refugees fleeing persecution should be treated as we would wish to be treated were our situations reversed. From a strictly egalitarian perspective, national boundaries appear to be vehicles for collective selfishness.

On the other hand, the founding document of the United States speaks of peoples as well as individuals, and of the "separate and equal station" to which the "laws of nature and of nature's God" entitle each people. In principle, not just individuals but also peoples stand in a relation of equality to one another, and these two kinds of equality can collide in practice. So can individual freedom and national self-determination.

Tribal Sentiments

A measure of tribalism seems hardwired in the human condition, and in the often unacknowledged sentiments of individuals. We take pleasure in associating with those who share our language, customs, and history, and we are more likely to trust them than to trust "outsiders." When resources are to be shared, we are likely to prefer those with whom we identify. When our tribe is challenged, our sense of identification strengthens, as does the impulse to come to its assistance. When transtribal commitments challenge tribal identification, the tribe usually prevails, as it did at the outset of World War I, when the vaunted international unity of the working class unceremoniously collapsed.

Populism is unambiguously and unashamedly tribal. It legitimates sentiments that liberal democratic principles suppress. This is one of its main sources of strength. Tribes ascribe merit to their members and inferiority to nonmembers, usually in stereotypical terms. This gives rise to the remarkably stubborn phenomenon of prejudice. Even when members of a tribe are persuaded through reason and experience that their prejudice is unwarranted, the sentiment persists. Populist politicians understand this and appeal to their supporters by giving voice to views elites regard as beyond the pale, gleefully violating a norm known in the United States as "political correctness." When leaders breach these restraints, it produces a sense of release for their followers, much as comedy does. It also encourages people to imitate their leaders, with dangerous consequences for individual security and social order.

In circumstances of scarcity or threat, the dyad of same and different gives way to the dyad of friends and enemies. Here too populism goes with the grain, liberalism against it. Antipathy, like concord, has its satisfactions. Life in rule-governed societies suppresses anger and aggression. Designating an enemy legitimates their release.

Hierarchy versus Equality

This is not to say that the citizens of liberal democracies have nothing to be angry about. Liberal democratic polities combine moral equality with economic and social inequality. When the wealth of economic elites seems disconnected from—even opposed to—the well-being of the community, the community reacts with moral indignation.

Inequalities of status are even more emotionally volatile. Every society, no matter how egalitarian in principle, has multiple social hierarchies. Those of higher status often look down on people lower on the status ladder, who answer disdain with resentment. Being denigrated, if only with a gesture or a glance, always stings. Being ignored is even worse.

In principle, liberal democratic societies accord social status based on achievement rather than the accident of birth. But individuals can achieve along many different dimensions, and the kinds of achievement a society singles out shape how it defines status. In contemporary liberal democracies, educational and professional achievement is especially prized. Individuals without such achievement often are made to feel second-rate, and they respond by dismissing claims based on expertise in favor of common sense and gut instinct.

Elite professional institutions such as the U.S. Federal Reserve Board are always exposed to this critique, all the more so if they are designed to be insulated from political influence. In such cases, economic and status concerns often merge, because it is natural to imagine that distant, secretive institutions serve the interests of the elites, not average citizens.

Action versus Constraint

Liberal democratic governance breeds many kinds of public frustration. Citizens elect representatives who do not—indeed, cannot —do what each voter wants, in part because voters support candidates for different, often opposing reasons. Citizens' desire to govern themselves collides with the obligations of daily life and also with most people's distaste for the practice of politics. "The trouble with socialism," Oscar Wilde is said to have remarked, is that "it takes too many evenings." So does every other political program, if one takes it seriously. Most citizens want government that is of the people and for the people, but they are ambivalent about government by the people.

Some liberal democratic systems divide power among multiple institutions, deliberately slowing decision-making to allow diverse points of view to participate in shaping policy. Multiparty parliamentary systems typically require parties to negotiate to form a government. Both these systems frustrate citizens' desire for swift, decisive action. Adding to their frustration, all liberal democratic regimes prevent majorities from acting when their desires collide with the rights of individuals and minority groups.

Liberal democratic societies require each citizen to share civic space with others of diverse views and hues, which is exhilarating for some but grating to others. Citizens are not called upon to agree with or like one another, but they are required to permit others to speak and act as they see fit, within broad limits. The desire to suppress speech and behavior one finds offensive is instinctive. Restraining oneself from doing so goes against the grain and requires training and indoctrination. Even when this process of social formation is successful, a residue of the desire to suppress difference remains, and the result is inner conflict. This is the specifically liberal democratic strand of the painful instinctual renunciation that Freud analyzed in *Civilization and Its Discontents*.[9]

States and Markets

I end with some reflections in the spirit of the late Robert Dahl. Liberal democratic political institutions cohabit with market economies, and I have argued that the latter are a necessary condition for the former. Not only do well-functioning market economies produce the prosperity needed to mute cultural conflict and class warfare, a partly independent sphere of property and transactions helps secure the individual liberty that liberal democratic politics pledges to defend.[10]

On the other hand, even regulated markets produce inequality, which beyond a certain point becomes a problem for democracy. Aristotle, the first political scientist, proposed a linkage between a strong middle class and a stable constitutional regime. So did James Madison.[11] Contemporary political science affirms this connection. When the trend toward inequality increases the demographic shares of the rich and the poor at the expense of the middle, conflict between the extremes is likely to intensify. And because economic resources can be translated into political power, the wealthy can exert disproportionate influence on public policy.

We can argue about whether, left to their own devices, market economies move inexorably toward wider inequality. But it is unarguable that beyond a certain point economic inequality is a threat to liberal democracy. From time to time, then, the political system must act to keep market outcomes within due democratic bounds.

There is no reason to believe that liberal democracy can ever permanently resolve the tension between state institutions and the market, in large measure because to some extent technological change happens independently of both politics and markets. The Industrial Revolution produced new economic formations that called for novel political responses. The results—universal suffrage, public regulation of corporations, and the development of social insurance—helped constrain economic inequality for many decades. Although the legacy of the Industrial Revolution continues to shape democratic politics throughout the West, relentless technological transformation in the context of globalization has raised new questions that inherited political institutions are less and less competent to address.

Of all the enduring problems of liberal democracy, the tension between politics and markets calls for the most creativity. It requires a thorough reexamination of long-held beliefs along with an expanded social imagination. As Abraham Lincoln said at a fateful juncture, "The dogmas of the quiet past, are inadequate to the stormy present. . . . As our case is new, so we must think anew, and act anew. We must disenthrall ourselves."[12]

In history's long view, liberal democracy's decisive advantage over other forms of government lies in its capacity for reinvention. Not just the United States but the entire West is being asked once more to exercise this capacity. This is a moral duty—and a practical necessity. As Lincoln reminded his fellow citizens, "We cannot escape history."[13]

Notes

Introduction

1. *Poorer Than Their Parents? Flat or Falling Incomes in Advanced Economies* (New York: McKinsey Global Institute, 2016), 4, available at http://www.mckinsey.com/global-themes/employment-and-growth/poorer-than-their-parents-a-new-perspective-on-income-inequality.

ONE
Democratic Erosion and Political Convergence

1. Michael J. Crozier, Samuel P. Huntington, and Joji Watanuki, *The Crisis of Democracy* (New York: New York University Press, 1975), available at http://trilateral.org/download/doc/crisis_of_democracy.pdf.
2. David Goodhart, *The Road to Somewhere* (London: Hurst, 2017).
3. Arch Puddington and Tyler Roylance, *Freedom in the World 2017—Populists and Autocrats: The Dual Threat to Global Democracy* (Washington, DC: Freedom House, 2017), 1 and 5, available at https://freedomhouse.org/sites/default/files/FH_FIW_2017_Report_Final.pdf.
4. Ibid., 4 and 1.
5. Patrick Chamorel, "The Political Right(s) in France," *American Interest* 11, no. 3 (Winter 2016): 27, available at https://www.the-american-interest.com/2015/09/28/the-political-rights-in-france/.
6. Ibid.

TWO

Liberal Democracy in Theory

1. *The Federalist Papers* (New York: Mentor Books, 1961), No. 39.
2. *The Federalist Papers*, No. 71.
3. *The Federalist Papers*, No. 63.
4. *The Federalist Papers*, No. 2.
5. Ibid.
6. Quoted in Graham Allison, "The Lee Kuan Yew Conundrum," *Atlantic*, March 30, 2015, https://www.theatlantic.com/international/archive/2015/03/lee-kuan-yew-conundrum-democracy-singapore/388955/.
7. Calvin Cheng, "The West Has It Totally Wrong on Lee Kuan Yew," *Independent*, March 26, 2015, http://www.independent.co.uk/voices/comment/the-west-has-it-totally-wrong-on-lee-kuan-yew-10135641.html.
8. Puddington and Roylance, *Freedom in the World 2017*, 23.
9. For the best short summary, see Robert A. Dahl, *On Democracy*, 2nd ed. (New Haven: Yale University Press, 2015).
10. Benjamin Constant, "The Liberty of the Ancients Compared with That of the Moderns," in *Constant: Political Writings*, ed. Biancamaria Fontana (Cambridge: Cambridge University Press, 1988), 102.
11. Ibid.
12. Benjamin M. Friedman, *The Moral Consequences of Economic Growth* (New York: Knopf, 2005), 4.

THREE

The Populist Challenge

1. For more on these topics, see Amanda Taub, "The Rise of American Authoritarianism," *Vox*, March 1, 2016, vox.com/2016/3/1/11127424/trump-authoritarianism; Jonathan Haidt, "When and Why Nationalism Beats Globalism," *American Interest* 32, no. 3 (Spring 2016): 46–53, available at https://www.the-american-interest.com/2016/07/10/when-and-why-nationalism-beats-globalism/; Stanley Feldman and Karen Stenner, "Perceived Threat and Authoritarianism," *Political Psychology* 18, no. 4 (December 1997): 741–70.
2. Jan-Werner Müller, *What Is Populism?* (Philadelphia: University of Pennsylvania Press, 2016), 10.
3. Cas Mudde, *Populist Radical Right Parties in Europe* (Cambridge: Cambridge University Press, 2007), 23.
4. Nativism often accompanies populism. The question is whether these two phenomena are inextricably intertwined and, if not, what nativism by itself means for liberal democracy. Takis Pappas argues, "Unlike populism, nativ-

ism does not work against political liberalism *for the natives.* Nativism's main arguments have to do with immigration and EU multiculturalism. Nativists see both as grave threats to well-ordered, ethnoculturally coherent societies, to their established liberal-democratic values, and, perhaps most crucially, to the sustainability of the welfare states that these societies have inherited from the days before mass immigration." There is something to this. Some people oppose Muslim immigration on the ground that Islam is incompatible with liberal respect for pluralism and with democracy itself. Some people oppose mass immigration from all sources because, they say, it weakens that sense of solidarity among citizens that undergirds the welfare state. It is unclear, however, what share of nativism is attributable to these relatively benign motives. See Takis S. Pappas, "Distinguishing Liberal Democracy's Challengers," *Journal of Democracy* 27, no. 4 (October 2016): 22–36, available at http://www.journalofdemocracy.org/sites/default/files/Pappas-27-4.pdf.

5. Mudde, *Populist Radical Right Parties in Europe,* 138; Cas Mudde, "The Problem with Populism," *Guardian,* February 17, 2015, https://www.theguardian .com/commentisfree/2015/feb/17/problem-populism-syriza-podemos-dark -side-europe.

6. Quoted in Jan-Werner Müller, "A Majority of 'Deplorables'?" *Project Syndicate,* November 10, 2016, https://www.project-syndicate.org/commentary/ trump-voters-opposition-to-democracy-by-jan-werner-mueller-2016-11.

7. Müller, *What Is Populism?* 77.

8. Ibid., 3.

9. Ibid., 9, 3, and 56.

10. Jeff D. Colgan and Robert O. Keohane, "The Liberal Order Is Rigged: Fix It Now or Watch It Wither," *Foreign Affairs* 96, no. 3 (May/June 2017): 36– 44, available at https://www.foreignaffairs.com/articles/world/2017-04-17/ liberal-order-rigged.

FOUR
The European Project and Its Enemies

1. Pope Francis, "Address of His Holiness Pope Francis to the Heads of State and Government of the European Union in Italy for the Celebration of the 60th Anniversary of the Treaty of Rome," March 24, 2017, available at http:// w2.vatican.va/content/francesco/en/speeches/2017/march/documents/papa -francesco_20170324_capi-unione-europea.html.

2. Mabel Berezin, "It's Time to Admit It: We're All Afraid of Terrorism— and That's the Entire Point of It," *Salon,* July 22, 2016, http://www.salon .com/2016/07/22/its_time_to_admit_it_were_all_afraid_of_terrorism_and _thats_the_entire_point_of_it_partner/.

3. Pope Francis, "Address"; Marine Le Pen, October 27, 2013, https://plus .google.com/+MarineLePen/posts/KMvEFQteEJe; Mabel Berezin, "Electoral Events as Collateral Damages: Sovereign Debt and the Old 'New' Nationalism in Post-Security Europe" (2014): 27, available at http://people.soc .cornell.edu/mmb39/BerezinEJSFinalDistributionCopyMay2014.pdf.

4. Cas Mudde, "Populist Radical Right Parties in Europe Today," in *Transformations of Populism in Europe and the Americas: History and Recent Tendencies*, ed. John Abromeit et al. (London: Bloomsbury, 2015), 295; Müller, *What Is Populism?* 6.

5. Roberto Stefan Foa and Yascha Mounk, "The Signs of Deconsolidation," *Journal of Democracy* 28, no. 1 (January 2017): 8, available at http://www.jour nalofdemocracy.org/sites/default/files/02_28.1_Foa%20%26%20Mounk %20pp%205-15.pdf; John Feffer, "Hungary's Economic Leap," republished in *Huffington Post*, May 23, 2014, http://www.johnfeffer.com/hungarys-eco nomic-leap/; Mitchell A. Orenstein, "Six Markets to Watch: Poland," *Foreign Affairs* 93, no. 1 (January/February 2014): 23, available at https://www .foreignaffairs.com/articles/poland/2013-12-06/six-markets-watch-poland.

6. Lidia Csizmadia, "The Transition Economy of Hungary between 1990 and 2004," M.Sc. finance diss., University of Aarhus, 2008, 40, available at http:// pure.au.dk/portal/files/2620/Csizmadia-Thesis.pdf page 40/; "Poland's Resurgent Right: Voting for a Better Yesterday," *Economist*, October 22, 2015, https://www.economist.com/news/europe/21676782-country-has-benefited -hugely-eu-membership-turns-bit-eurosceptic-voting-better.

7. In this same address, Orban stated that the EPP coalition to which Fidesz adheres is not populist. "We should not be afraid of leftist criticism calling us populists. We know, we are not," Orban declared. On the other hand, he affirms populist premises and practices. He seems to embrace the populist vision while rejecting the label. See Speech of Viktor Orban at the EPP Congress, March 30, 2017, available at http://www.miniszterelnok.hu/speech-of -viktor-orban-at-the-epp-congress/.

8. Jan-Werner Müller, "Viktor Orban Is Europe's Enemy Within," *Financial Times*, April 10, 2017, https://www.ft.com/content/4d4bd9a2–1dc6–11e7 -b7d3–163f5a7f229c.

9. Richard Wike, Bruce Stokes, and Katie Simmons, *Europeans Fear Wave of Refugees Will Mean More Terrorism, Fewer Jobs* (Washington, DC: Pew Research Center, 2016), 8, available at http://www.pewglobal.org/2016/07/11/ europeans-fear-wave-of-refugees-will-mean-more-terrorism-fewer-jobs/; *Religious Belief and National Belonging in Central and Eastern Europe* (Washington, DC: Pew Research Center, 2017), 154, available at http://www.pew forum.org/2017/05/10/religious-belief-and-national-belonging-in-central -and-eastern-europe/; Dorothy Manevich, "Hungarians Share Europe's Embrace of Democratic Principles but Are Less Tolerant of Refugees, Minori-

ties," *Pew Research Center,* September 30, 2016, http://www.pewresearch.org
/fact-tank/2016/09/30/hungarians-share-europes-embrace-of-democratic
-principles-but-are-less-tolerant-of-refugees-minorities/; Slawomir Sierakowski, "The EU Has a Moral Obligation to Act against Poland," *Financial Times,*
July 19, 2017, https://www.ft.com/content/f7c7474e-6bc9-11e7-b9c7-15af7
48b60d0.

10. Quoted in Mitchell A. Orenstein, "Paranoid in Poland: How Worried Should the
West Be about the Law and Justice Party's Victory?" *Foreign Affairs,* November 1, 2015, https://www.foreignaffairs.com/articles/poland/2015-11-01/para
noid-poland?cid=soc-tw-rdr; quoted in Nick Gutteridge, "Shock as Hungary PM Says Migrants Are 'Poison' and EVERY Refugee a 'Safety & Terror
Risk,'" *Express,* July 27, 2016, http://www.express.co.uk/news/world/693994/
Hungary-PM-Viktor-Orban-migrants-refugees-poison-terror-risk.

11. Elizabeth Collett, "Why Poland Wants Container Camps for Asylum Seekers," *Foreign Affairs,* May 4, 2017, https://www.foreignaffairs.com/articles/
poland/2017-05-04/why-poland-wants-container-camps-asylum-seekers.

12. Müller, *What Is Populism?* 45 and 48; Ellen Hinsey, *Mastering the Past: Contemporary Central and Eastern Europe and the Rise of Illiberalism* (Candor, NY:
Telos Press, 2017), 100.

13. Sierakowski, "The EU Has a Moral Obligation to Act against Poland."

14. While near majorities in Hungary and Poland prefer democracy to other
forms of government, about a quarter think nondemocratic government is
preferable in some situations. Those without college educations are more
likely to hold agnostic attitudes toward democracy. See *Religious Belief and
National Belonging in Central and Eastern Europe.*

15. Quoted in Hinsey, *Mastering the Past,* 102.

16. Quoted in Müller, *What Is Populism?* 26; quoted in "Poland's Resurgent
Right"; quoted in James Traub, "The Party That Wants to Make Poland
Great Again," *New York Times,* November 2, 2016, https://www.nytimes.com/
2016/11/06/magazine/the-party-that-wants-to-make-poland-great-again
.html?_r=0.

17. John Shattuck, "Resisting Trumpism in Europe and the United States,"
American Prospect, December 2, 2016, http://prospect.org/article/resisting
-trumpism-europe-and-united-states.

18. Ivan Krastev, "The Unraveling of the Post-1989 Order," *Journal of Democracy*
27, no. 4 (October 2016): 13, available at http://www.journalofdemocracy
.org/sites/default/files/Krastev-27-4.pdf.

19. Quoted in Hinsey, *Mastering the Past,* 71–72.

20. Krastev, "The Unraveling of the Post-1989 Order," 10.

21. Quoted in Hinsey, *Mastering the Past,* 132.

22. Quoted in ibid., 103; quoted in Remi Adekoya, "Xenophobic, Authoritarian,
and Generous on Welfare: How Poland's Right Rules," *Guardian,* October

25, 2016, https://www.theguardian.com/commentisfree/2016/oct/25/poland -right-law-justice-party-europe.

23. Quoted in "Far-Right Hopeful: French Election 'Choice of Civilization,'" *AP News*, February 5, 2017, https://www.apnews.com/e94cf5ff5bc342a5b5e 13fd227d083dc; quoted in Adam Nossiter, "Marine Le Pen Echoes Trump's Bleak Populism in French Campaign Kickoff," *New York Times*, February 5, 2017, https://www.nytimes.com/2017/02/05/world/europe/marine-le-pen -trump-populism-france-election.html?_r=1.

24. Conrad Hackett, "5 Facts about the Muslim Population in Europe," *Pew Research Center*, July 19, 2016, http://www.pewresearch.org/fact-tank/2016/07/19/5 -facts-about-the-muslim-population-in-europe/; John Irish, "French Far Right Uses Halal Accusation to Woo Voters," *Reuters*, February 19, 2012, http://www.reuters.com/article/us-france-election-lepen-idUSTRE81 I06920120219; Kim Willsher, "France's Muslims Hit Back at Nicolas Sarkozy's Policy on Halal Meat," *Guardian*, March 10, 2012, https://www .theguardian.com/world/2012/mar/10/nicolas-sarkozy-halal-meat-france -election.

25. Cécile Alduy, "The Battle for the Soul of France," *Nation* 298, no. 12 (March 2014): 20–21, available at https://www.thenation.com/article/has-marine-le -pen-already-won-battle-soul-france/; Aurelien Mondon, "The French Secular Hypocrisy: The Extreme Right, the Republic and the Battle for Hegemony," *Patterns of Prejudice* 49, no. 4 (2015): 402, available at http://www.tandfonline .com/doi/abs/10.1080/0031322X.2015.1069063?journalCode=rpop20.

26. Yves Bertoncini and Dídac Gutiérrez-Peris, *Nothing to Fear but Fear Itself? France* (London: Demos, 2017), 137, available at https://www.demos.co.uk/ wp-content/uploads/2017/02/Demos-Nothing-To-Fear-But-Fear-Itself .pdf.

27. Mondon, "The French Secular Hypocrisy," 398.

28. Timothy Snyder, "The Reichstag Warning," *New York Review of Books*, February 26, 2017, http://www.nybooks.com/daily/2017/02/26/reichstag-fire-ma nipulating-terror-to-end-democracy/.

29. Arthur Goldhammer, "Explaining the Rise of the Front National: Political Rhetoric or Cultural Insecurity?" *French Politics, Culture & Society* 33, no. 22 (Summer 2015): 141, available at http://www.berghahnjournals.com/view/ journals/fpcs/33/2/fpcs330208.xml?.

30. Ibid., 135; Alduy, "The Battle for the Soul of France," 21 and 19.

31. Cas Mudde, *Populist Radical Right Parties in Europe*, 119–20; Abel Mestre, "'Sudiste' et 'nordiste,' les deux électorats du FN," *Le Monde*, July 8, 2013, http://www.lemonde.fr/politique/article/2013/08/07/face-nord-et-face -sud-les-deux-electorats-du-fn_3458468_823448.html.

32. Alduy, "The Battle for the Soul of France," 21.

33. Quoted in Mabel Berezin, *Illiberal Politics in Neoliberal Times: Culture, Se-*

curity, and Populism in the New Europe (Cambridge: Cambridge University Press, 2009), 246, 244, and 248.

34.   Quoted in Alduy, "The Battle for the Soul of France," 20.

35.   Ibid., 21.

36.   Mondon, "The French Secular Hypocrisy," 397; Berezin, "Electoral Events as Collateral Damages," 16.

37.   Quoted in May Bulman, "Marine Le Pen Refuses to Repay €300,000 in 'Misspent' EU Funds," *Independent,* February 1, 2017, http://www.independ ent.co.uk/news/world/europe/marine-le-pen-european-parliament-funds -eu-misspent-front-national-france-a7556771.html; quoted in Nicholas Vinocur, "Marine Le Pen Makes Globalization the Enemy," *Politico,* February 5, 2017, http://www.politico.eu/article/marine-le-pen-globalization-campaign -launch-french-politics-news-lyon-islam/.

38.   *2nd tour présidentielle 2017: Comprendre le vote des Français* (Paris: Ipsos, 2017), 11, available at http://www.ipsos.fr/sites/default/files/doc_associe/sondage _ipsos_soprasteria_-_6_mai_19h.pdf.

39.   *Standard Eurobarometer 85—European Citizenship* (Brussels: European Commission and Directorate-General for Communication, 2016), 18, available at http://ec.europa.eu/COMMFrontOffice/publicopinion/index.cfm/Survey/ getSurveyDetail/instruments/STANDARD/surveyKy/2130; Galina Zapryanova and Neli Esipova, "Most in Eastern Europe Positive about EU Membership," *Gallup,* May 10, 2017, http://www.gallup.com/poll/210083/eastern -europe-positive-membership.aspx.

40.   Alan Finlayson, "Imagined Communities," in *The Blackwell Companion to Political Sociology,* ed. Kate Nash and Alan Scott (Oxford: Blackwell, 2001), 290.

41.   Quoted in Hinsey, *Mastering the Past,* 103.

42.   Pierre Manent, "Populist Demagogy and the Fanaticism of the Center," *American Affairs* 1, no. 2 (Summer 2017), available at https://americanaffairs journal.org/2017/05/populist-demagogy-and-the-fanaticism-of-the-center/.

FIVE

Is Democracy at Risk in the United States?

1.   Ralph Scott, Charlie Cadywould, Sacha Hilhorst, and Louis Reynolds, *Nothing to Fear but Fear Itself? Great Britain* (London: Demos, 2017), 55, available at https://www.demos.co.uk/wp-content/uploads/2017/02/Nothing-to-Fear -but-Fear-Itelf-final.pdf.

2.   Unpublished materials from research by Matthew Goodwin and Oliver Heath, *Brexit Vote Explained: Poverty, Low Skills, and Lack of Opportunities* (York: Joseph Rowntree Foundation, 2016), available at https://www.jrf.org .uk/report/brexit-vote-explained-poverty-low-skills-and-lack-opportunities.

3. Kirby Swales, *Understanding the Leave Vote* (London: NatCen Social Research, 2016), 10, available at http://natcen.ac.uk/media/1319222/natcen_brexplanations-report-final-web2.pdf; Scott, Cadywould, Hillhorst, and Reynolds, *Nothing to Fear but Fear Itself? Great Britain*, 60, 54, 59, and 61; Sascha O. Becker, Thiemo Fetzer, and Dennis Novy, "Who Voted for Brexit? A Comprehensive District-Level Analysis," Centre for Economic Performance Discussions Paper No. 1480, October 2017, 29, http://cep.lse.ac.uk/pubs/download/dp1480.pdf.

4. Matthew Goodwin and Oliver Heath, "A Tale of Two Countries: Brexit and the 'Left Behind' Thesis," London School of Economics and Political Science British Politics and Policy blog, July 22, 2016, http://blogs.lse.ac.uk/politicsandpolicy/brexit-and-the-left-behind-thesis/.

5. Becker, Fetzer, and Novy, "Who Voted for Brexit?" 32.

6. Scott, Cadywould, Hillhorst, and Reynolds, *Nothing to Fear but Fear Itself? Great Britain*, 81.

7. "How the United Kingdom Voted on Thursday . . . and Why," *Lord Ashcroft Polls*, June 24, 2016, http://lordashcroftpolls.com/2016/06/how-the-united-kingdom-voted-and-why/.

8. Swales, *Understanding the Leave Vote*, 19.

9. Scott, Cadywould, Hillhorst, and Reynolds, *Nothing to Fear but Fear Itself? Great Britain*, 66.

10. Ibid., 83.

11. Isabel V. Sawhill and Eleanor Krause, "Incomes Are Rising, but It's too Soon to Celebrate," Brookings Institution's Social Mobility Memos blog, September 20, 2016, https://www.brookings.edu/blog/social-mobility-memos/2016/09/20/incomes-are-rising-but-its-too-soon-to-celebrate/.

12. *Inside the Middle Class: Bad Times Hit the Good Life* (Washington, DC: Pew Research Center, 2008), available at http://www.pewsocialtrends.org/2009/03/26/iv-trends-in-household-income-1970-2007/.

13. "Rural Employment and Unemployment," *United States Department of Agriculture Economic Research Service*, July 6, 2017, https://www.ers.usda.gov/topics/rural-economy-population/employment-education/rural-employment-and-unemployment/.

14. Economic Innovation Group, cited in Thomas B. Edsall, "Reaching Out to the Voters the Left Left Behind," *New York Times*, April 13 2017, https://www.nytimes.com/2017/04/13/opinion/reaching-out-to-the-voters-the-left-left-behind.html.

15. See especially David H. Autor, David Dorn, and Gordon H. Hanson, "The China Shock: Learning from Labor-Market Adjustment to Large Changes in Trade," *Annual Review of Economics* 8 (2016): 205–40, available at http://www.annualreviews.org/doi/pdf/10.1146/annurev-economics-080315-015041.

16. Raj Chetty et al., "The Fading American Dream: Trends in Absolute Income

Mobility Since 1940," National Bureau of Economic Research, Working Paper 22910, December 2016, 18, http://www.nber.org/papers/w22910.pdf.

17. Bruce Stokes, *Global Publics: Economic Conditions Are Bad* (Washington, DC: Pew Research Center, 2015), 10, available at http://www.pewglobal.org/2015/07/23/global-publics-economic-conditions-are-bad/.

18. Ibid.

19. William A. Galston, "Immigration Reaches Critical Mass," *Wall Street Journal*, November 22, 2016, https://www.wsj.com/articles/immigration-reaches-critical-mass-1479857623.

20. Ruy Teixeira, William H. Frey, and Robert Griffin, *States of Change: The Demographic Evolution of the American Electorate, 1974–2060* (Washington, DC: States of Change, 2015), 3, available at https://cdn.americanprogress.org/wp-content/uploads/2015/02/SOC-report1.pdf.

21. *ABC News/Washington Post* poll, June 20–23, 2016, and *NBC News/Wall Street Journal* survey, June 19–23, 2016, available at http://pollingreport.com/terror.htm.

22. Bill Bishop, *The Big Sort: Why the Clustering of Like-Minded America Is Tearing Us Apart* (New York: Houghton Mifflin, 2008).

23. *Partisanship and Political Animosity in 2016* (Washington, DC: Pew Research Center, 2016), 51, 3, and 5, available at http://www.people-press.org/2016/06/22/partisanship-and-political-animosity-in-2016/.

24. Robert P. Jones, Daniel Cox, E. J. Dionne Jr., William A. Galston, Betsy Cooper, and Rachel Lienesch, *How Immigration and Concerns about Cultural Changes Are Shaping the 2016 Election* (Washington, DC: Public Religion Research Institute and Brookings Institution, 2016), 23–24, available at https://www.prri.org/wp-content/uploads/2016/06/PRRI-Brookings-2016-Immigration-survey-report.pdf.

25. Emily Ekins, *The Trump Voter Typology* (Washington, DC: Democracy Fund Voter Study Group, 2017), 10–14, available at https://www.voterstudygroup.org/reports/2016-elections/the-five-types-trump-voters.

26. Ibid., 6 and 11–15.

27. Ibid., 15; John Sides, *How Race, Religion, and Immigration Mattered in 2016—and What That Means for a Trump Presidency* (Washington, DC: Democracy Fund Voter Study Group, 2017), 5-6, available at https://www.voterstudygroup.org/reports/2016-elections/race-religion-immigration-2016.

28. Sides, *How Race, Religion, and Immigration Mattered in 2016*, 12.

29. See especially Daniel Cox, Rachel Lienesch, and Robert P. Jones, *Beyond Economics: Fears of Cultural Displacement Pushed the White Working Class to Trump* (Washington, DC: Public Religion Research Institute and The Atlantic, 2017), available at https://www.prri.org/research/white-working-class-attitudes-economy-trade-immigration-election-donald-trump/.

30. Robert Griffin and Ruy Teixeira, *The Story of Trump's Appeal: A Portrait of*

Trump Voters (Washington, DC: Democracy Fund Voter Study Group, 2017), 18–19 and 23–24, available at https://www.voterstudygroup.org/reports/2016-elections/story-of-trumps-appeal.

31. *Beyond Distrust: How Americans View Their Government* (Washington, DC: Pew Research Center, 2016), 18, available at http://www.people-press.org/2015/11/23/beyond-distrust-how-americans-view-their-government/.

32. *Public Trust in Government Remains Near Historic Lows as Partisan Attitudes Shift* (Washington, DC: Pew Research Center, 2017), 1, http://www.people-press.org/2017/05/03/public-trust-in-government-remains-near-historic-lows-as-partisan-attitudes-shift/.

33. *Beyond Distrust*, 26.

34. *NBC News/Wall Street Journal* polls, 1995–2016, http://www.pollingreport.com/right.htm.

35. Roberto Stefan Foa and Yascha Mounk, "The Danger of Deconsolidation," *Journal of Democracy* 27, no. 3 (July 2016): 5–17, available at http://www.journalofdemocracy.org/article/danger-deconsolidation-democratic-disconnect; Roberto Stefan Foa and Yascha Mounk, "The Signs of Deconsolidation," *Journal of Democracy* 28, no. 1 (January 2017): 5–15, available at http://www.journalofdemocracy.org/article/signs-deconsolidation.

36. *The 2015 State of the First Amendment* (Washington, DC: Newseum Institute, 2015), 14, available at http://www.newseuminstitute.org/wp-content/uploads/2015/07/FAC_SOFA15_report.pdf.

37. Franklin D. Roosevelt, "Inaugural Address," March 4, 1933, available at http://www.presidency.ucsb.edu/ws/?pid=14473.

38. See especially Agnes Cornell, Jørgen Møller, and Svend-Erik Skaaning, "The Real Lessons of the Interwar Years," *Journal of Democracy* 28, no. 3 (July 2017): 14–28, available at http://www.journalofdemocracy.org/sites/default/files/03_28.3_M%C3%B8ller%20%28web%29.pdf.

SIX

Liberal Democracy in America

1. "Wilson, Charles E.," GM Heritage Center, https://history.gmheritagecenter.com/wiki/index.php/Wilson,_Charles_E.

2. William A. Galston, *The New Challenge to Market Democracies: The Political and Social Costs of Economic Stagnation* (Washington, DC: Brookings Institution, 2014), 13, available at https://www.brookings.edu/research/the-new-challenge-to-market-democracies-the-political-and-social-costs-of-economic-stagnation/.

3. For an elaboration of the argument see Jim Kessler, "Why Not Growth?" *Third Way*, August 4, 2014, http://www.thirdway.org/op-ed/why-not-growth.

4. Edmund Burke, *Reflections on the Revolution in France* (Garden City, NY: Doubleday, 1961), 110.
5. *Politics of Aristotle*, trans. Benjamin Jowett (Oxford: Clarendon Press, 1885), 18.
6. *The Broadview Anthology of Social and Political Thought: From Plato to Nietzsche*, ed. Andrew Bailey, Samantha Brennan, Will Kymlicka, Jacob Levy, Alex Sager, and Clark Wolf (Toronto: Broadview Press, 2008), 109.
7. Colgan and Keohane, "The Liberal Order Is Rigged," 44.
8. Alice M. Rivlin, "A New Vision of American Federalism," *Public Administration Review* 52, no. 4 (July–August 1992): 315–20.
9. Quoted in Emily Heil, "Mark Twain on Congress," April 18, 2012, https://www.washingtonpost.com/blogs/in-the-loop/post/mark-twain-on-congress-idiots-criminals-dumber-than-fleas/2012/04/18/gIQA3J4nQT_blog.html?utm_term=.c009a154f765.
10. Bo Rothstein, "Why Has the White Working Class Abandoned the Left?" *Social Europe*, January 19, 2017, https://www.socialeurope.eu/white-working-class-abandoned-left.
11. Interview with Ezra Klein, "Francis Fukuyama: America Is in 'One of the Most Severe Political Crises I Have Experienced,'" *Vox*, August 26, 2016, https://www.vox.com/2016/10/26/13352946/francis-fukuyama-ezra-klein.
12. *The Federalist Papers* (New York: Mentor Books, 1961), No. 47.
13. Bo Rothstein, "The Long Affairs between the Working Class and the Intellectual Cultural Left Is Over," *Social Europe*, February 10, 2017, https://www.socialeurope.eu/long-affair-working-class-intellectual-cultural-left.
14. The locus classicus of this argument is John B. Judis and Ruy Teixeira, *The Emerging Democratic Majority* (New York: Scribner, 2002). In fairness, both Judis and Teixeira have since rethought their positions, and neither would advocate strategic neglect of the white working class.

SEVEN

Democratic Leadership

1. Aristotle, *Politics*, trans. Carnes Lord (Chicago: University of Chicago, 1984), 43.
2. Quoted in Richard E. Neustadt, *Presidential Power and the Modern Presidents: The Politics of Leadership from Roosevelt to Reagan* (New York: Free Press, 1991), 10.
3. Aristotle, *"Art" of Rhetoric*, trans. J. H. Freese (Cambridge, MA: Harvard University Press, 1967), 89.
4. For a vivid account, see "The British Royal Visit: June 7–12th, 1939," FDR Presidential Library and Museum, available at https://fdrlibrary.org/royal-visit.

5. John Kane and Haig Patapan, *The Democratic Leader: How Democracy Defines, Empowers and Limits Its Leaders* (Oxford: Oxford University Press, 2012), 3 and 14.

6. *The Federalist Papers* (New York: Mentor Books, 1961), No. 39.

7. *The Federalist Papers*, No. 68.

8. Thomas Jefferson to John Adams, October 28, 1813, available at http://press-pubs.uchicago.edu/founders/documents/v1ch15s61.html.

9. William A. Galston, "Populist Resentment, Elitist Arrogance: Two Challenges to Good Democratic Leadership," in *Good Democratic Leadership: On Prudence and Judgment in Modern Democracies*, ed. John Kane and Haig Patapan (Oxford: Oxford University Press, 2014), 20.

10. Kane and Patapan, *The Democratic Leader*, 32–33.

11. Ibid., 56.

12. *The Federalist Papers*, No. 55.

13. William Shakespeare, *Coriolanus*, act II, scene iii, available at http://shakespeare.mit.edu/coriolanus/full.html.

14. Quoted in George Charles Mitchell, *Matthew B. Ridgway: Soldier, Statesman, Scholar, Citizen* (Mechanicsburg, PA: Stackpole Books, 1999), 90–91.

15. Ronald Reagan, "Acceptance Speech at the 1980 Republican Convention," July 17, 1980, available at http://www.presidency.ucsb.edu/ws/index.php?pid=25970.

16. For a concise narrative, see National Archives, "Documents Related to Brown v. Board of Education," www.archives.gov/education/lessons/brown-v-board.

17. William Shakespeare, *Julius Caesar*, act IV, scene iii, available at http://shakespeare.mit.edu/julius_caesar/julius_caesar.4.3.html.

18. See Howard Jones, *Abraham Lincoln and a New Birth of Freedom: The Union and Slavery in the Diplomacy of the Civil War* (Lincoln: University of Nebraska Press, 1999), 146.

19. *The Federalist Papers*, No. 57.

20. For parallel accounts of this episode, see Basil Rauch, *Roosevelt from Munich to Pearl Harbor* (New York: Creative Age Press, 1950), 267; and David Reynolds, *From Munich to Pearl Harbor: Roosevelt's America and the Origins of the Second World War* (Chicago: Ivan R. Dee, 2001), 101.

EIGHT
The Incompleteness of Liberal Democracy

1. Quoted in Albert O. Hirschman, *The Passions and the Interests* (Princeton: Princeton University Press, 1977), 134.

2. Quoted in ibid., 106–7.

3. Quoted in Roland N. Stromberg, *Redemption by War: The Intellectuals and 1914* (Lawrence: Regents Press of Kansas, 1982), 186.
4. This is not to deny that more personal elements (including a failed romance) also shaped Brooke's outlook.
5. Quoted in Stromberg, *Redemption by War*, 9.
6. Quoted in ibid., 191.
7. Erich Fromm, *Escape from Freedom* (New York: Henry Holt, 1994).
8. Quoted in Stromberg, *Redemption by War*, 88.
9. Sigmund Freud, *Civilization and Its Discontents* (Peterborough, Ontario: Broadview Press, 2015).
10. Dahl puts it this way: "Polyarchal democracy has endured only in countries with a predominantly market-capitalist economy" and "this strict relation exists because certain basic features of market-capitalism make it favorable for democratic institutions." Dahl, *On Democracy*, 166–67.
11. In a remarkable 1792 letter, Madison observed that the difference of material interests is the greatest source of party divisions and urged policies that would mitigate these divisions. Among the steps he recommended are "laws which, without violating the rights of property, reduced extreme wealth toward a state of mediocrity and raised extreme indigence toward a state of comfort." See *Liberty and Order: The First American Party Struggle*, ed. Lance Banning (Indianapolis: Liberty Fund, 2004), 104.
12. Abraham Lincoln, "Annual Message to Congress," December 1, 1862, available at http://www.presidency.ucsb.edu/ws/?pid=29503.
13. Ibid.

Index

Index

Spain, 42
stagnation, economic, 15, 18, 32, 34, 57, 59, 68, 92
steel mills, 12, 79, 80
Supreme Court (U.S.), 25, 79, 80–81, 107, 118–19
Syriza (Greece), 42

taxes, 79, 87, 88, 89, 92, 95, 98, 99
technological change, 10, 15, 84, 91, 103, 135–36
terrorism 16, 56, 72, 80, 95; populist response to, 43, 44, 47, 55, 71
Thatcher, Margaret, 8
Third Way, 8–9, 86
tolerance, 6, 32, 113, 127
trade, 9, 10, 13, 69
traditionalism, 3, 13–14, 22, 46
transparency, 98, 112
Treasury (U.S.), 99
tribalism, 42, 77, 128, 132
Truman, Harry, 80, 106, 116
Trump, Donald, 39, 64, 67, 73, 78, 80, 81, 111; presidential campaign, 11–12, 17, 37, 69, 71, 95, 102, 104; rise of, 77; supporters, 74–76, 124–25
Tspiras, Alexis, 42
Twain, Mark, 98
tyranny, 1, 30, 52, 82, 101, 114, 115

unemployment, 3, 9, 46, 57, 70, 75, 88; in Europe, 15, 31, 91
unions. *See* labor unions
United Kingdom, 3, 11, 17, 40, 42, 54, 66. *See also* Britain; England
United Kingdom Independence Party, 64

United States, 63, 74, 78–79, 102, 103, 136; Constitution, 26, 27, 93, 131; constitutional system, 11, 73, 79, 81, 111, 116; democracy, 12, 80–81; economy, 9, 15, 31, 69, 83, 84–85; immigration, 3, 10, 71, 76, 96; political culture, 107, 108; political system, 97, 98; populism in the, ix, 11, 40, 67, 101, 102, 113, 117. *See also* election, presidential (U.S., 2016)
urban centers, 68. *See also* cities; metropolitan areas
urban-rural divide, 2–3, 11, 15, 45, 68, 89, 90

Venezuela, 23, 93, 112
Vietnam War, 74
Vinson, Fred, 118

Warren, Earl, 118–19
Washington consensus, 9, 91
welfare, 7, 8, 9, 42. *See also* social protections
Wilde, Oscar, 134
Willkie, Wendell, 123
Wilson, Charles, 84
working class, 3, 5, 56, 65, 70, 79, 93, 103; disaffection of, 15, 18, 54, 57; white (in U.S.), 74, 78, 103
World Trade Organization, 18, 69
World War I, 31, 128–29, 132
World War II, 7, 14, 18, 41, 74, 84, 90; economic growth following, 3, 15, 31, 83

xenophobia, 45, 76, 103

Yeats, William Butler, 130